Fearless Swimming for Triathletes

Dedication

To McKayla, who overcame her fear of sharks in the bathtub, the pool and the ocean too.

For better readability, we have decided to use the masculine (neutral) form of address, but the information also refers to women.

Ironman Edition

Fearless Swimming
for Triathletes

IMPROVE YOUR OPEN WATER SKILLS

Ingrid Loos Miller

Meyer & Meyer Sport

3 1257 02375 8245

IRONMAN® is a registered trademark of World Triathlon Corporation

British Library Cataloguing in Publication Data
A catalogue record for this book is available from the British Library

Fearless Swimming for Triathletes
Maidenhead: Meyer & Meyer Sport (UK) Ltd., 2011
ISBN 978-1-84126-120-1

© 2011 by Meyer & Meyer Sport (UK) Ltd.
Auckland, Beirut, Budapest, Cairo, Cape Town, Dubai, Graz, Indianapolis, Maidenhead,
Melbourne, Olten, Singapore, Tehran, Toronto
Member of the World
Sport Publishers' Association (WSPA)
www.w-s-p-a.org
Printed and bound by: B.O.S.S Druck und Medien GmbH, Germany
ISBN 978-1-84126-120-1
E-Mail: info@m-m-sports.com
www.m-m-sports.com

© Bakke-Svensson/Ironman

Contents

INTRODUCTION

It's all over their faces – that deer-in-the-headlights look – when a new triathlete utters the "S" word. Swim.

Athletes are chipped, numbered, capped and corralled then set loose at the pull of a trigger. It is every man (and woman) for himself. Paddlers, jet skis, boats, and kayaks are everywhere with lifeguards keeping watch. However, despite these safety measures, triathletes have died during the swim. If you have done a triathlon, you understand how it could happen.

Every triathlete feels the rush of adrenaline. Every triathlete gasps when plunging into the cold water and every triathlete has to overcome the anxiety of looking into pea soup and wondering what is down there. Imaginations run wild and heart rates plummet then soar. Body contact is heavy and unexpected blows are startling. The throat spasms and, for a moment, you just... can't... breathe! Those new to swimming have this to overcome and more. Propulsion in the water does not come naturally when you learn to swim as an adult. There are DVDs, books and coaches to smooth the way but, like learning a foreign language, becoming a swimmer comes infinitely easier to the young.

No matter how much a triathlete trains and races, some will always consider themselves poor, nervous swimmers. Many have had bad experiences in the water. Some are just sinkers. If you are one of these people, this book is for you.

This book is also for swimmers who suffer a kind of discombobulation when they get into open water, even though they are fine in the pool. For these swimmers, their apprehensions are limited to race day.

Finally, this book is for swimmers who are fine everywhere but in the ocean, which is exceptionally threatening with her waves, currents and creatures.

By necessity, this book says a lot about the difficulties and dangers of triathlon swimming. When I was writing, I kept having to remind myself that the book is called Fearless Swimming. Writing about being elbow-deep in sudden death and shark attacks made me think the book should be called How to Die in a Triathlon instead, but there is no way around it. The truth must be told, and happily, dangerous incidents in triathlon swimming are very rare.

It goes with the territory that you can't talk about managing a fear without shining light on it with frank discussion. I figure if you are interested in this book, you have already imagined some awful scenarios and are aware of the unfortunate accidents that have occurred. That said, it is tremendously helpful and worthwhile to bathe your senses in the beauty and serenity that open water swimming offers. Except for a passage by distance swimmer extraordinaire Lynne Cox, you won't get much of that here.

This book will help you understand what is dangerous about triathlon swimming and how to manage what scares you most. No matter what your experience level, I hope you learn something that will make your next race better.

— **Ingrid**

Disclaimer

This book contains the author's interpretation of research and some discussions with professionals in the field. It is also based upon the author's personal experiences. The author has attempted to present material that will be helpful to readers, but it should not be considered medical or therapeutic advice. The author is not a physician, psychologist or psychiatrist, nor has she had any formal training in these fields.

The information in this book should be viewed as an introduction to the subject from one layperson to another. Readers should use their own discretion about when and whether to try any of the actions suggested in this book. Readers are encouraged to explore the author's suggestions more deeply on their own before following any advice that may make them uncomfortable or that may subject them to danger.

Section 1:
Fearless Swimming Tools

You are fearless when you recognize
why you should be scared of things,
but you go out and do them anyway.

THE FEARLESS SWIMMING TOOLS

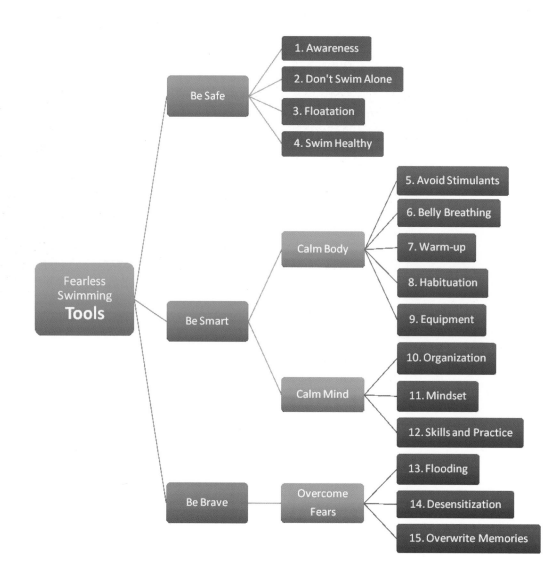

The number that identifies each tool (1-15) on the chart is also used in the book where it is first discussed. The application of these tools is described in various contexts throughout the book.

© Bakke-Svensson/Ironman

CHAPTER 1
How to Become a
Fearless Swimmer

The swim should be the easiest, most comfortable part of your race.
If it isn't, you've got work to do.

-Fearless swimmer

WHY IS THE SWIM SO HARD?

Don't feel bad. You are not alone. In a 2004 survey, Ironman athletes identified swimming and the mass start as the one of their biggest concerns. Specific fears included "drowning," "surviving the swim," and "too many overzealous competitors that knock you silly in the swim to gain a meter" (1). An internet search for "triathlon panic swimming" will bring enough hits to demonstrate how common these difficulties are. You can spend days reading forum postings on the subject, and you may be tempted to add your own stories but don't; commiserating with others may be comforting, but it won't move you forward.

To become a fearless swimmer, strive to make swimming your "Zen" event. See it as an *escape* from stress. On training days at least, it should be meditative, pure and joyful. It should also be the easiest, most comfortable part of your race. That may sound like a lofty goal, but it can be achieved with focus, practice and patience. Becoming a Fearless Swimmer is the goal, not the starting point.

You are reading this book because, for now, swimming is a source of stress, not an escape from it. Some things about it may terrify you (like mass starts) and others you may find annoying (like getting water in your nose). I call all of these difficulties "Fear Factors". The ones in Box 1 are addressed in this book. Which ones apply to you?

Triathlon swimming is a jackpot of stress. Your wetsuit is too tight, you are all packed in like sardines, you have to put your face into cold murky water and look into the shadowy abyss. You don't know how deep it is, and you don't know what's down there. You can't see where you are going. About 2 minutes into the

Box 1. Fear Factors

- Panic Attacks
- Dizziness
- Difficulty Breathing
- Asthma Attacks
- Embarrassment
- Bad Memories
- Heart Attack /Sudden Death
- Drowning
- Tight Wetsuit
- Claustrophobia
- Hyperventilation
- Muscle Cramps

- Seasickness
- Murky Water
- Navigating
- Sharks
- Mob Swimming
- Mass Starts
- Currents & Chop
- Waves
- Riptides
- Polluted Water
- Cold Water

race, you realize you aren't getting enough air. Anxiety turns to panic when you get a mouthful of water instead of air. You tell yourself to relax and breathe deep, but then you hyperventilate and get dizzy. Are you going to make it through the swim? Fear of losing control, panicking or embarrassing yourself are ever-present threats. What if you have to be rescued? On top of this, you may have had a swim-related trauma that haunts you and, oh yes, you need to go fast too.

In a race there are many factors that contribute to your stress level. It may seem like the whole situation is out of control but as you read on, you will be surprised at the number of factors *you can control* with information, learning new skills and selective practice. By distinguishing the things you can control from the things you can't, you can spend your time where it will help you the most.

FEAR

Fear is an emotion generated by a combination of physiology (body reactions) and cognition (thought reactions). These reactions are so closely tied that the line between them sometimes gets blurry. The physical and mental reactions fuel each other (see Figure 1.). The good news is that you can learn to control some of them. Every step you take to reduce the reactivity of your body and mind will reduce your stress level, moving you closer to achieving fearless swimming.

Figure 1. *Fear is generated by physical and mental responses that feed on each other. The tools and skills described in this book address both sources of fear.*

DEALING WITH PANIC

The term "panic attack" has been used to describe the fear and lack of control some people may experience under extreme stress. People with panic disorder describe attacks as among the worst experiences in their lives. Part of the problem is that the attacks come on suddenly for no apparent reason. This makes the syndrome especially difficult because suffers don't know when an attack will appear (2). The panic that you may experience in a race may be frightening but is probably not technically a panic attack because it happens in response to a stressful situation. It is predictable, preventable and escapable once it begins.

If your anxiety is so bad that you are starting to avoid racing entirely, you may be within the realm of true panic and you should find help beyond this book. The self-assessment questionnaire in Appendix A can help you decide if your anxiety level justifies intervention. If you think you may suffer true panic attacks, get help from a professional.

FOCUS ON THE FUN

Open water swimming is only as hard as you make it. The right perspective and frame of mind are key. Before we get into the nuts and bolts of becoming a fearless swimmer, read what long-distance champion Lynne Cox has to say about her first open water race:

"We stood shoulder to shoulder along the shore, an official fired the starting gun, and we ran across the beach and dolphined under the waves. The water was cold, salty, buoyant, smooth and the deepest blue. And I swam as if I had learned to fly.

I raced across the water. My strokes felt powerful, and I felt strong, alive as if awakened for the first time. Nothing in the swimming pool gave me this pleasure. I was free, moving fast, feeling the waves lifting and embracing me, and I couldn't believe how happy I was. It was like I had gone from a cage into limitless possibilities. With each stroke, my own strength grew; I felt the speed, the wake my body created.... It was such a tremendous sensation, as if I had found my place, finally, found my niche in the universe.

I swam with all my heart and found myself passing one swimmer after another. I am really going somewhere. I am really moving forward. I lifted my head up, and I could see the oil rig that represented the halfway point in the distance, about a mile away.

I couldn't believe I had swum so fast, but there was nothing holding me back. There were no walls, no black lines to follow, no lane lines or backstroke flags; I was surrounded by the wide-open sea and the infinite sky filled with puffy white clouds.

Before I knew it, I rounded the large white buoy in front of the oil rig and started my return to shore. I felt currents tugging me first in one direction, then the other, and I wondered with great fascination how the currents moved, how they chose a direction.

Everything was new, fresh, alive, and wonderful. The water played like music around my head, my shoulders shimmered in the sunlight and I grew stronger, my strokes became more powerful. I went faster and faster, catching more swimmers, delighted with everything" (3).

As you work through this book, remember Lynne's perspective. Adopt the mindset that what you are doing is fun and, no matter what, act as if it is. Focus on the fun, not the fear, and you will be on your way to becoming a fearless swimmer.

GETTING STARTED

If you are a beginner, *being well prepared for your first triathlon swim is more important than any other aspect of your first race*. Doing your homework will help you enjoy the swim instead of dreading it. If you have to delay your first race because you aren't quite ready, do so.

Before you do a triathlon, you have to know how to swim, and you have to be confident that you could swim much farther than the upcoming race distance with relative ease.

MASTERS SWIMMING IS NOT REQUIRED

In the context of competitive swimming, Masters Swimming groups are clubs and teams of adults who train together and compete in swim meets. Much of what you read implies that to be a good swimmer, you have to swim with a Masters group. Maybe that is true if you want to be fast for swim meets or you want to ramp up your speed work, but Masters swimming is not necessarily the best use of your time if you need help with your stroke or you want to work on open water skills. Plenty of adults have had to learn to swim from square one.

Beginners need personal, one-on-one attention to reach a level of competence and ease with their swimming technique before worrying about speed intervals. Being able to swim 100 yards/meters in 2 minutes or less with ease is a reasonable starting point for your first triathlon.

Improving technique should be an ongoing process. The principles of Terry Laughlin's Total Immersion program are excellent for everyone, but especially for new and nervous swimmers. His books and DVDs are designed to help swimmers work on their own to refine technique. Make a habit of going through the material at the beginning of every race season and using some of the drills in every warm-up. Over time, you will continue to improve.

SWIMMING SOLO

I have been a swimmer my whole life. I am proficient and comfortable in the water, but I have to admit that every time I get into the pool for lap swim while the Masters Group is practicing, I break out in a sweat and my heart starts racing. The social element of feeling like you are being judged is an undeniable truth that exists at every level.

Since the goal here is to make swimming your Zen event, it is worthwhile to make it as comfortable and stress-free as possible. If you have to drive a bit farther or pay a higher pool fee in order to have an uncrowded, stress-free swim experience, do it. For safety reasons, you should always have someone around when you swim, but it doesn't have to be an entire swim team. Swimming with friends is fun too, but find a way to be in your own space mentally when you train. Building a foundation of peacefulness and comfort in the water will speed your learning.

WEAR YOUR WETSUIT

New triathletes often complain about feeling anxious in their wetsuits. This is either because their wetsuit doesn't fit right, or they haven't practiced in it enough. If you plan to wear your wetsuit at your first race then it makes sense to swim in it at least half a dozen times before race day. In fact, wearing your wetsuit as you learn to swim and refine technique is a more relevant aid to learning than paddles and kickboards.

The advantages are many, as long as you don't get overheated. Even in a warm pool on a warm day, you can do a few hundred easy yards in your wetsuit. It is also ideal for drill work that is not very strenuous. Wearing a wetsuit makes you more buoyant, and this keeps your legs from dragging, which is a common difficulty for new swimmers. The improved body position makes it easier to learn other aspects of technique.

ANONYMITY

Fear of embarrassment is among the most powerful human fears. It shackles your enjoyment of the learning process. Just getting out there on race day can be overwhelming. Don't worry. Triathletes have more anonymity than most athletes. On race day, you will melt into the mass as soon as you don your wetsuit, cap and goggles so don't fret too much about it. You will be just another wetsuit in the crowd.

If you have to stop and rest on a paddleboard, no one on shore will know it's you (other than your mom who can pick you out of a crowd a mile away). The lifeguard won't know who you are either. You can be rescued, dragged to shore and given oxygen and still no one will be the wiser when you are in street clothes. Feel free to experiment without being self-conscious. No one really cares about what you are doing anyway. They are too busy worrying about their own performance.

PATIENCE

Signing up for a race before you are prepared may motivate you, but don't paint yourself into a corner time-wise. It is important and worthwhile to prepare well for your races. Pick one that is far enough in the future to give you adequate preparation time.

Stress and time pressure are enemies of fearless swimming. Work on one skill at a time before moving to the next one. Acknowledge incremental success. Triathlon is like an onion. There are many layers of skill and experience that go into the sport. It takes time to form each layer.

EDUCATION

Reading about a scary subject is unpleasant. If you have a highly reactive nervous system, simply *reading* about motion sickness will make you nauseous and reading about sharks will make your heart pound. It may seem that, for some problems, the best way to overcome them is to pretend they don't exist. It is

certainly easier. But skillful mental gymnastics don't get you very far. At some point, you have to face your fear if you want to overcome it.

It is imperative to separate myth from fact. Psychologists call this truth testing, and it is a vital step in the process of overcoming fear. Some Fear Factors are truly dangerous, like big surf or coronary artery disease. Knowing something about those things can save your life. Other fears, like staying out of the ocean because you fear a shark attack or being afraid of looking into dark water are more psychological than real (depending on the circumstances) and facts don't seem as helpful. However, in both cases, reading about the things that scare you is a safe, simple first step to exposing yourself to the fear, which is part of overcoming it.

If you go all out and immerse yourself in the feared subject, you may initially become even more anxious about it, but eventually you will get used to it, get bored and move on. Getting bored with something that scares you is a gigantic step in the right direction.

PRACTICE, PRACTICE

Once you can swim well enough, you should learn all of the fearless swimming skills in Section 2. A checklist of the skills is in Appendix E. Use the fearless swimming tools to help you address your personal Fear Factors as you work through the skills. Master all of the skills, even if they seem easy for you. Practice is essential.

The surf-specific skills are necessary only for ocean racing. The more surf skills you acquire, the better. Bodysurfing and riding a riptide are not required for ocean competence, but they sure help.

© Bakke-Svensson/Ironman

CHAPTER 2
Be Safe, Be Smart, Be Brave

In this chapter, you will be introduced to the fearless swimming tools listed at the beginning of this section. These are the tools that will help you deal with your Fear Factors. Ways to use them will be discussed throughout the book.

BE SAFE

Fearless swimming begins with feeling safe in the open water. No matter where you are, basic safety rules apply and you probably already know them. Below are some that are particularly relevant to nervous swimmers in open water.

TOOL #1: AWARENESS

You have probably been to your local pool so many times that you can picture the location of every pool drain and tile. One of the things that makes pool swimming so much easier than open water is the predictability of the environment. You can take for granted that the water is warm and safe.

When you swim in open water, the environment can change rapidly and dangers are not necessarily obvious. The water might be contaminated or rocks may be submerged just under the surface of the water, so be careful about diving in head-first. When swimming in open water, you should go through a mental checklist to make sure the area is safe before you dive into the water. We will discuss those checklists in detail later.

TOOL #2: DON'T SWIM ALONE

Being alone in a large body of water makes you feel vulnerable; a reaction that is natural. But no one said you had to swim alone to be a fearless swimmer; and it isn't safe either. Swim and practice the fearless swimming skills near other people. If there is a lifeguard, swim near her. If not, you should have a buddy watch you from the shore, swim with you or paddle alongside in a kayak. You should also keep a cell phone handy on shore and, of course, know CPR.

One advantage of race day is that you will never feel lonely. It is safer to swim with others so take advantage of group swimming opportunities. Participate in swims hosted by triathlon clubs and participate in pre-race swims and clinics at race venues. The more you swim in open water, the better.

TOOL #3: FLOATATION

It is pretty hard to sink in a wetsuit, but if you want extra security and a nice place to rest, consider swimming with a foam rescue tube like the ones used by lifeguards. These devices have a shoulder strap so you can swim freely while dragging the buoy behind. If the line slips off your shoulder, you can tie it around your waist instead. They don't cost much and are widely available online. If you swim in open water with a group, it is a good idea for someone to wear one of these tubes, especially if there is no lifeguard around.

TOOL #4: SWIM HEALTHY

Confirm that you are physically up to the task of training for and racing triathlons. The unfortunate deaths that have occurred in triathlon swims are a sober reminder that danger can lurk undetected, even for athletes. In later chapters, you will learn about these dangers and what to watch out for. Pay attention to symptoms, don't swim with a fever and have annual physical examinations including an EKG to rule out dangerous cardiac conditions.

BE SMART

A calm body and a peaceful mind make for a fearless swimmer.
Preparing your body for triathlon swimming should go beyond physical conditioning. There are specific exercises that can reduce your reactivity to cold water, motion and poor visibility. Avoiding stimulants, investing in your warm-up and knowing how and when to use breathing techniques will moderate your physical response to stress. When your body is less stressed, it is easier to stay calm.

Peace of mind will come more easily when you are organized and have a successful mindset with goals that move you toward becoming a fearless swimmer (before you worry about being a fast one). Focusing strategies and achieving competence in the fearless swimming skills in Section 2 will boost your confidence.

CALM YOUR BODY

TOOL #5: AVOID STIMULANTS

Caffeine temporarily increases activity of the sympathetic nervous system and releases adrenaline, which is part of the fight or flight response to stress. Beware of chocolate, colas, energy drinks and over-the-counter medications that contain caffeine. Don't consume more than 100 mg/day of caffeine (1 cup of coffee or 2 colas) if you are prone to anxiety (1). Avoiding caffeine and other stimulants, like amphetamines and ginseng, are an easy way to reduce your fear response on race day.

TOOL #6: BELLY BREATHING

An awareness of your breathing is one of the first symptoms of stress. Likewise, controlling respiration is one of the most effective ways to relieve

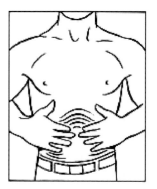

stress. Diaphragmatic or "belly breathing" (BB) is a simple and versatile stress management tool. It will effectively slow the heart rate, reduce anxious feelings and can even reduce seasickness (Figure 2).

Breathing out (exhaling) with the diaphragm

Figure 2. Belly breathing.
Source: US.Army Medical Dept. Office of Medical History.

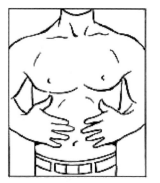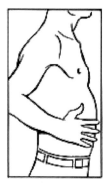

The trick is to slow your breathing way down. Inhale gently but deeply into your belly (not your chest) every 12 seconds or so. At the same time, say to yourself: "One, Anxiety. Two, Won't Die. Three, Just. Breathe. Slow." See Figure 3.

Breathing in (inhaling) with the diaphragm

Anxiety.   **Won't Die.**   **Just. Breathe. Slow.**

Figure 3. 1-2-3 Thoughts. Adapted from Howtogetridofthings.com

Belly breathing allows the chest muscles to relax, which helps the feeling of breathlessness go away (2, 3). As you calm down, your heart rate will go down, too. Try the experiment in Box 2 to confirm the effect of this technique on your own heart rate.

Box 2. Belly breathing experiment

Put on your heart rate monitor and get a baseline heart rate when you are alone in a quiet place. Then have someone come into the room and make annoying sounds and watch your heart rate go up. Begin the breathing exercises and see how long it takes for your heart rate to go down again.

Breathing Breaks

USAT rules allow athletes to stop and rest during the swim, so if you see a kayak or paddler nearby, you can float on it and take a belly bretahing break. You can also just stop and tread water. The only limitation of this technique is that you can't do it while you are actually swimming. To be best prepared, you should practice the technique on land, in the pool and in open water. It works quickly, and soon you will be on your way again.

You can build breathing breaks into training swims and races. These are akin to taking walk breaks during a long run. It reduces the intensity of your effort, allows your heart rate to go down and keeps you in control. It is especially helpful in the first 5 to 10 minutes of the race. Let's face it, you see competitors do this all the time, but very few of them have *planned* it. Planning makes all the difference in the world, emotionally. Remember, you are just another athlete in a wetsuit so don't worry about being embarrassed. You will end up going faster than the people who start out too fast and flounder around exhausted for the last half of the swim.

Start with counting strokes as soon as the gun goes off. Take a breathing break at about 100 strokes. Make sure you are well off to the side so you don't block other swimmers behind you. When you feel relaxed and in control, resume swimming. Repeat this cycle as needed. If you are feeling good, increase the number of strokes between breaks. Eventually, you will not need breaks at all.

Use the belly breathing technique when you do the exposure exercises described below. Combining the breathing technique with the exercises makes them more effective.

TOOL #7: INVEST IN YOUR WARM-UP

Warming up for the swim is crucial, but too many athletes either rush through it or skip it altogether. It is so important that you should not only do it, you should *invest* in it — spend time. But how long? When you swim in the pool, how long do you have to swim before you are completely relaxed and the blood is flowing nicely? It is probably close to 10 minutes. Ten minutes is the minimum.

Warming up allows your body to go through the entire cycle of cold water shock, exertion, and disorientation before you are under performance pressure. The warm-up is also an opportunity to find your sighting landmarks and adjust them if necessary. Confirm that you are wearing the right goggles. At the end of your warm-up, you should be able to put your head in the water and swim in a relaxed state.

Use belly breathing and create a calm mindset to bring your heart rate down before the race if you get jittery. The warm-up is required to quiet your body and mind before you get to the starting line. Do it well and often and your races will go more smoothly.

TOOL #8: HABITUATION

When you first get dressed, you feel the clothing against your skin but after a few minutes you are no longer aware of them. This is known as "habituation" in scientific circles, and it is a physiological learning process. It means getting used to something, and it is important because when your body is used to something, it is less reactive. Reducing reactivity helps you deal with Fear Factors more easily.

Habituation is useful in many contexts. Habituation programs have been developed and widely used by the military to help their pilots get over motion sickness without the use of drugs that make them drowsy. A sample habituation program for motion sickness appears in Chapter 3. The exercises in Chapter 10 will help you deal with looking through murky water. Acclimiation is also an effective way to adjust to cold water.

Habituation programs (like desensitization) are a progression of movements that bring you slowly to a point of stress then you back off and recover. Next, you start at the beginning again and proceed through the progression and hopefully you can go further. The goal is to slowly raise your tolerance for disturbing movements before reaching the point of stress until eventually you can tolerate all of the movements.

TOOL #9: EQUIPMENT

Having the right equipment goes a long way to improving your comfort and effectiveness in the water. There is no need to suffer with dizziness if earplugs will solve the problem. If you can't deal with water in your nose, maybe a nose clip is worthwhile. Throughout the book, I will make suggestions about several items that will help you. The next chapter is about one of the most important pieces of equipment, your wetsuit.

CALM YOUR MIND

Fearless swimmers have quiet minds. Being organized eliminates a predictable source of race day stress.

TOOL #10: ORGANIZATION

Race Reconnaissance
The more familiar you are with the race venue, the lower your anxiety level will be. Study the course maps and use online maps to get 3D views and photos. Visit the venue if you can.

Race reconnaissance should yield the following information:

- The location of T1 relative to the swim start: How far away is it? What kind of terrain (sand, shells, rocks)? Is there a hill to T1?
- Water temperature: Is it cold enough for a wetsuit? Will neoprene socks and cap be helpful?
- Weather forecast: Will it be warm, windy, raining or foggy on race day?
- Start location: Will you start from deep water, a beach, boat or dock?
- Landmarks: What are the large landmarks you can use for navigation?
- Finish location: Beach, stairs, or dock?
- Pre-race swim: If you have the opportunity before race day, get in the water and do your warm-up. Is the water clear?

Pre-race Checklist

Incorporate your race reconnaissance into a pre-race checklist. Such a list will reassure you that you have everything you need on race day. Here is an example of a pre-race checklist for the swim:

- Race schedule or timeline including wake-up time, breakfast, travel time, time to set up T1, time to warm up and when to get to the starting line.
- Warm clothes to wear during check-in and transition set-up. Will you wear your running shoes?
- Sunscreen
- Wetsuit or Skinsuit
- Race cap
- Neoprene cap and/or socks if needed
- Body Glide or other lubricant
- Goggles and spares in various tints
- Timing chip on your ankle

It helps to have a list like this that will apply to your entire race, so it should include everything you need for all three disciplines. Save the list on your computer so you don't have to reinvent it and you can customize it for each race.

TOOL #11: MINDSET AND FOCUS

Mindset is a broad term that encompasses goals and focusing strategies that help you deal with particular situations. There are times when focusing on what makes you afraid is important, like when you are working on overcoming a particular fear. At other times, it is important to distract yourself by focusing on an object or a mental task that will help you keep fearful thoughts away.

Below is a description of these strategies and how to use them. Practice them in training so you have a variety to choose from on race day. Use them whenever you think they will help you.

Opposite Goals

Goals are your own creations, and the right ones are entirely within your control. Everyone is familiar with time goals (wanting to finish the swim in a certain time). You have also probably heard of process goals. Process goals are about the specific things you need to do (e.g., technique, keeping a certain cadence, etc.) that will ultimately help you reach your time goal.

Process goals are usually better than time goals because the process is much more in your control than a particular finish time. Time goals depend a lot on weather and environmental factors that you can't control.

But there is another kind of goal too, an opposite goal. Imagine if your goal on race day was to be the most relaxed finisher in the swim, regardless of time. Would the swim be easier? What if your plan was to take at *least* _____ (fill in a pathetically slow time) minutes to finish the swim. I call these opposite goals because they are designed to slow you down, not speed you up. For fearful swimmers, speed equals stress. If you want to overcome the stress, you have to teach yourself to race with relative calm. Doing this has all sorts of benefits, but the main one is that it reinforces your sense of control. How would you race differently if you created some opposite goals?

• You might seed yourself in a different location at the start.
• Perhaps you would wait a bit longer to get into the water once the gun goes off.
• Would you focus less on the mob and more on your own relaxation?
• Would you take a few moments to ensure the buoy was clear so you could go around it without getting crushed by others?
• What would your internal dialogue be?

The thought of racing without, well, *racing* sounds strange but it is *your* race. You pay the entry fee so you should *create the experience that is most valuable to you*. Yeah, you want to be fast, and with time and practice, you will be. But first, you have to deal with your swimming issues (Fear Factors). Do a race or two to before considering time goals.

Count Strokes

Lifting your head to look around is hard on your vestibular system, which is connected with balance and ultimately involved in motion sickness. The less you lift your head, the more at ease you will feel. Count strokes when you swim and make a game out of increasing the number of strokes between each head lift. Lifting your head every 40 strokes feels better than lifting it every five. When you learn some of the navigation tools, it will be easier to keep your head down longer. Counting strokes also slows and lengthens your stroke, improving efficiency as you relax and glide more. It is terrific for improving your swim times.

When you have a long swim, you can count strokes to break the swim into more manageable segments. For example, if you usually swim 20 strokes per lap in the pool and you have an Olympic distance race (66 lengths), you know you will take about 20 x 66 or 1,320 strokes to get to the finish line. To cut that down to four segments, each segment will be 330 strokes. All you have to do is count to 330, four times.

You will find that as you swim harder it is natural to count fewer and faster. When you can only count to four before starting again, you are probably exerting a maximum effort.

Watch Your Hands
As your hand enters the water and extends forward, it reaches a point of maximum extension, known as the target. This is where your catch begins. Watching your hands reach their target gives you a visual point of reference when there is no black line to look at. This will reduce the feeling of disorientation that contributes to motion sickness. Looking at your hands is also comforting.

To see your hands, you may have to change your head position slightly, from looking straight down to looking slightly ahead. This modified position has another advantage in that it allows you to sneak a peek at the buoy in front of you without moving your head as much. Practice in the pool to find a comfortable head position that allows you to see your hands (or at least your arms).

Bird's Eye View
View the race from a different vantage point to distract and calm you. Imagine a bird's eye view of the race. All the swimmers start moving along in a pack, then they begin to spread out. See the swimmers, then pan away and peruse the race venue and the town. Now slowly zoom back. Look at the lead swimmer, then find yourself in the pack swimming strong and smooth.

Removing yourself from the race in this way is an effective way to focus on the bigger picture of what you are doing rather than on how green the water is.

Mind Video
Create in your mind a personal video that captures the sensation of swimming so quietly that the water hardly ripples as you slice lightly through it. Scour the internet for videos and images of beautiful, graceful swimming. Add images of the light dancing off the bottom of the pool and music to the rhythm of your unhurried breathing. Recite a favorite mantra if your music doesn't have lyrics. Put the music, images and sensations together like a lullaby and play it in your mind when you do your warm-up in the pool. Practice it in open water, too. Use

it regularly and make it a pleasant ritual that you can use on race day for your warm-up and beyond.

You can also use an existing video. Explore the internet for movie segments or videos of perfect swimmers set to music. Play the video during your race to keep you focused on the pleasure of swimming.

Distraction

From a performance standpoint, it is best to focus on your technique during a race. But if you are really scared, focusing on something other than swimming can get you through.

You can create what is known as inattentional blindness by focusing your mind on a challenging task. When the mind is fully engaged, you don't see the other things that are happening. This is the kind of thing that happens when you talk on the cell phone while driving. Although your eyes see the road, your mind doesn't. Many aspects of your surroundings go unnoticed (4).

Research has shown that participating in a conversation is an effective way to create inattentional blindness. If you could talk on your cell as you swim, you would be less afraid, wouldn't you? Although you can't actually do this (yet), you can do it in your imagination. Come up with some scenarios before you get into the water and try them out. For example, imagine:

1. Having a conversation with a favorite teacher. Tell her what you have done with your life so far.
2. Explaining how to shift gears to someone who has never ridden a bike before.
3. Interviewing your favorite movie star, historical figure or athlete.

If a conversation doesn't work, try these cognitive tasks:

1. Organize your family into alphabetical order.
2. Solve a math problem.
3. Recite a childhood story from memory.

It does not matter what you think of, just make it a task that requires your ongoing attention and focus. Your mind will be so engaged with the task that it will be less reactive to the immediate environment. When driving, this is a bad thing; but for a nervous swimmer, it can be magic.

TOOL #12: SKILLS AND PRACTICE

This book teaches you the tools to keep you calm and the skills you need for open water success, but you have to practice them all.

First, use the tools to calm your body: avoid stimulants, belly breathe, invest in your warm-up, habituate to cold and murky water, and get the right equipment. Second, practice with the tools to calm your mind. Try the various mindset and focus strategies so you know which ones work for you.

Next, use these now-practiced strategies as you learn the fearless swimming skills. You should learn the skills first in the pool where you feel at ease.

Once you have mastered the fearless swimming skills in the pool (along with the calming strategies), you will be ready to practice them in the open water.

Do a race distance training swim at least twice before race day. Wear your wetsuit and do it in open water if you can. Nothing will boost your confidence more than doing the real thing.

With training you can become a stronger, faster triathlete and a more courageous one too. Bravery can be learned by acquiring skills and practicing them, so practice, practice, practice (6).

BE BRAVE

OVERCOME YOUR FEAR FACTORS

Psychologists say that one of the most effective ways to get over a fear is to expose yourself to the thing that scares you. That takes courage! Research suggests that do-it-yourself exposure is almost as effective as therapist-aided exposure, so it is worth a try (5). Exposure exercises are even more effective when you combine them with belly breathing.

For this section, we will use fear of deep water as an example. There are two kinds of exposure — fast and all at once, like jumping into the middle of a deep lake, or slow and a little at a time, like starting on the beach and venturing gradually into the water. Doing it fast is known as flooding and doing it slowly is known as desensitization. Flooding seems to work better, but it depends on what the fear is, how intensely you react to it, and whether there is danger involved (6).

TOOL #13: FLOODING

Flooding is putting yourself into the feared situation (jumping in the lake), focusing your mind on the fear (letting yourself be scared), and staying put for about 30 minutes in spite of your fear or until it subsides (6).

Flooding = Action (fear) + Engagement (focusing on the fear) + Staying Put

Getting into the feared situation is one thing, but focusing on the fear is also necessary. Distraction is a good way to temporarily avoid what scares you, but it will not help you overcome the fear (6). It is advisable to have a trusted friend accompany you. But the friend has to be able to resist the urge to "rescue" you (if you are in no danger) when you get scared. If you get out of the water in a panic, the fear will be even stronger (4). Once you jump in, you are committed.

Flooding can be applied to various fears. This technique may be helpful if you are afraid of swimming in the ocean because of sharks, afraid of murky water or get claustrophobic in your wetsuit. If you are afraid of swimming in the surf, you can use flooding once you have learned the basic skills and if you choose a safe time and location with mild surf.

Flooding is a high stakes game that requires a strong will. Plan carefully so you don't endanger yourself or others.

TOOL #14: DESENSITIZATION

Desensitization is the process of taking small, slow steps toward your Fear Factor. Desensitization like habituation, but habituation is getting your *body* used to something. Desensitization is about your *mind*.

Desensitization = Action + Action + Action + Action (approaching fear)

Desensitization takes awhile, and you should be mentally engaged (thinking about the fear) during the process so that you learn to face your fear both mentally and physically. The steps should be as small as necessary so that you can do them. Box 3 has an example. You should stop as soon as you begin to feel anxious, and do not proceed further until you feel calm again.

Box 3. Example of desensitization steps for overcoming fear of deep water

Step 1: Think about deep water and draw a picture of it.

Step 2: Read about people swimming in deep water.

Step 3: Look at photos of people swimming in deep water.

Step 4: Look at videos of people swimming in deep water.

Step 5: Go to a lake, and look at the water from shore.

Step 6: Get into a boat and look at the deep water from the middle of the lake.

Step 7: Put your feet in the water.

Step 8: Wade to your waist.

Step 9: Swim in water you can stand in.

Step 10: Swim in progressively deeper water.

Step 11: Get into a boat, go out into the middle of the lake and jump in.

Desensitization allows retreat, which makes it more palatable than flooding (which requires you to stay put and overcome your fear all at once) as a method of self-exposure. The principle of learning in a safe environment then progressing to a more challenging one is how the fearless swimming skills are structured in Section 2. It is the way we learn many complicated things, a little at a time.

Ease Into Racing

Races create an urgency and performance pressure that is hard to duplicate among friends in a pool. How do you create a race environment? The easy answer is to enter races, but that deprives you of the small steps that are necessary for desensitization to work. It is expensive, too. Here are some ways to ease into triathlon racing:

1. If you aren't ready to race yet, go to a local race and do a warm-up with the participants. Wear your wetsuit and goggles, and get into the water. Swim around until you feel comfortable, then relax and enjoy the race from the sidelines. Watch the swimmers closely and put yourself mentally in the race. What would your sighting landmarks be? What would you tell yourself if you were out there? How many swimmers stop and rest? How often do the lead swimmers raise their heads and look around?

2. Try a triathlon with a pool swim to introduce yourself to the sport while you enjoy the safety of the pool.

3. Short open water swimming races (in flat water) are excellent skill-builders. You can focus on the swim without the added pressure of a bike ride and run afterwards.

4. Enter a small triathlon with a short, flat swim. Enlist the help of a skilled and confident friend who is willing to stay with you during the entire swim. Talk to the race director or the lifeguards. At times, there are special caps given to new swimmers alerting the lifeguards to direct special attention to you.

5. Triathlon relays are a fun introduction to the sport. Do the swim leg of a relay in a short triathlon.

6. Do not sign up for an ocean triathlon without knowing whether or not there is surf at the venue! Start with small races that have very short swims in flat water.

TOOL #15: REPLACE BAD MEMORIES

Some of the anxiety connected with open water swimming is caused by cold-water immersion, compression from a wetsuit, limited vision, dizziness and exertion. When bad experiences or scary thoughts are added to these sensations, your brain puts the two together (association) and the fear becomes connected to open water swimming. The stronger your emotions are when the memories are made, the more resilient the memories are. When parts of the brain are bathed in stress hormones, memories are particularly vivid and difficult to shake.

Intense negative memories can turn into phobias, which are extremely difficult to overcome. People with water-related phobias are probably not triathletes, but fear doesn't have to be as bad as a true phobia to be troubling.

How do you disconnect your bad memories from open water swimming? It is easier to make new connections than to disable old ones. One approach is to create new open water experiences that are pleasant (5). But that isn't enough. These new experiences will only stick (be strong enough to rival the bad memories) if your emotions are involved. A pleasant way to get the emotions involved is to do something surprising, exciting and fun. But how do you do that? It is like trying to plan your own surprise party. It just won't work. The next best thing is to do something unique, preferably with a good-natured friend who thinks you are totally nuts.

Box 4 offers an example of how to create a new memory. Balloons add necessary novelty and fun. Consider other props like spray string, a Whoopee Cushion, squirt guns and noisemakers. Sounds like a party doesn't it?

Box 4. Balloon activity that can replace a bad memory associated with murky water

If you have a bad memory associated with swimming in murky water, you can help yourself by creating a novel murky water experience.

Find an open water venue with murky water (which shouldn't be difficult). Bring a friend, if you like, and half a dozen small, inflated balloons. Put your wetsuit on so you are comfortable and get into the water. Splash water on your face and neck and get your body used to the temperature. Put your face into the water and open your eyes. So far, so good. Now pull a balloon underwater (it is difficult to do) and pop it. Squeeze it under your arm or between your knees. If that doesn't work, you may have to resort to biting or pinching it. Do whatever it takes to pop it.

If you are with a friend, have a contest. Who can pop three balloons underwater the fastest? Loser has to buy the winner a new pair of goggles.

From then on, you will think about the balloon escapade every time you get into murky water. This weird experience will take center stage, and the bad memories will fade.

© Bakke-Svensson/Ironman

CHAPTER 3
Solve Annoying Problems

WATER IN THE NOSE

Getting water up your nose every time you breathe is no picnic. This may seem like a minor issue, but there is no reason to add it to your list of swimming discomforts. Athletes who swam with nose clips as kids sometimes have a hard time managing without them as adults. Athletes with sinus problems seem to suffer with this, too. There are two solutions: either swim with a nose clip or learn to swim without one.

If you want to learn to master swimming without a nose clip, allow a few weeks and plenty of practice to train yourself to keep water out of your nose as you swim. The exercises in Box 5 should help.

Box 5. Exercises that develop breathing coordination

Exercise 1:

Fill a bowl with water. Begin exhaling only through your nose and slowly put your face into the water. As you run out of air, lift your head straight out of the water as you continue to exhale. Don't stop blowing air out your nose until your face is completely clear of the water. Take a breath, then start again. A few drops of water may come out your nose as you start exhaling again. As you continue to exhale, put your face in the water again and repeat the process. If you get more water in your nose than you like, exhale forcefully and blow the drops out.

The crucial skill here is to begin exhaling before you put your face in the water and also while you are removing it. If you stop exhaling too soon, the water goes in. Humming should expel just enough air through your nose to keep the water out. Practice this every day until you master it.

Exercise 2:

This adds another step. Once your face is in the water, turn it to the side as you continue to exhale. Lift your head out of the water in that position, continuing to exhale.

Exercise 3:

Building on the previous exercises, instead of lifting your head completely out of the water, keep one ear submerged as you exhale. Then inhale only through your mouth. Begin exhaling through the nose and turn your face down into the water again. Practice doing this on both sides. As you progress, try to keep your face more deeply submerged in the water as you turn your head. Ultimately, you want to be able to turn your head just enough to get a breath. This exercise will help you build coordination for bilateral breathing, which is an important skill.

Exercise 4:

Now you are ready to try it in the pool. Sit on the stairs or bend at your waist and repeat the exercises above as you stand in the pool. When you have mastered them, incorporate what you have learned into your swimming — exhale through the nose before and after your face breaks the surface and inhale through the mouth.

If you work on this consistently, you will succeed. If you find that swimming without a nose clip is just too difficult, go ahead and wear one. Like goggles, nose clips come in various styles and colors, and they have different pinch levels, too. Experiment and find the ones that work best for you. Just make sure you are capable of swimming without them in case they get knocked off during a race.

EXERCISE ASSOCIATED MUSCLE CRAMPS (EAMC)

Everyone knows the feeling that comes right before a cramp. In scientific circles, it is known as "the cramp prone state," and it is like a warning sign. Only, by the time you get the warning, it is already too late. One false move and yipes! There goes your calf, hamstring or even your toe, and no matter how hard you try, you are out of the race until it goes away. Exercise associated muscle cramps (known as EAMC) are especially common in triathletes during the swim (1).

There is evidence that EAMC is brought on by circumstances *other* than electrolyte (e.g., salt, potassium or magnesium) shortage or dehydration. A 2005 study compared Ironman triathletes who had muscle cramps during the race with those who did not. Blood was drawn after the race to see if there were differences in electrolyte levels and other factors. The researchers found no significant differences between the two groups in their blood chemistry. The researchers concluded that muscle cramping is not associated with clinically significant differences in serum electrolyte concentrations (2). So what causes the cramps?

A growing body of research suggests that EAMC is caused by abnormal neuromuscular control in response to fatiguing exercise. This "muscle fatigue" theory is based on evidence from epidemiological studies, animal experimental data and electromyogram data recorded during bouts of acute cramping after fatiguing exercise (2, 3).

If you suffer from muscle cramps during the swim, it is most likely related to exercise but there are other disorders that can cause cramping, as well. Muscle cramps may be a symptom of radiculopathies, Parkinson's disease, hypothyroidism, diabetes mellitus, vascular problems, electrolyte disorders, and metabolic myopathies. They can also occur as a side effect of certain drugs, including lipid-lowering agents, antihypertensives, beta-agonists, insulin, oral contraceptives and alcohol (4).

Here is a list of factors that seem to play a role in exercise associated muscle cramping (5,6,7,8):

- Endurance events, such as marathons and triathlons, and especially first-time Ironman racers.
- Hot and humid conditions, but cold as well, especially for swimmers.
- Increasing exercise intensity. Cramps are more likely during a race than when training. A study of Ironman athletes showed that faster athletes were more likely to suffer EAMC, independent of how much they prepared or their performance history.
- Self-reported poor conditioning for the event.
- Later stages of the race.
- Increased exercise duration.
- Depletion of muscle energy stores.
- Sustained maximal muscle contraction with the muscle in a shortened position.
- Previous history of EAMC.
- Familial history of EAMC.

PREVENTION

What can be done to prevent cramps during the swim?
1. Condition the involved muscles adequately.
2. Eat and drink enough before the race.

CONDITIONING EXERCISES

Conditioning should be race specific. We know that cold water is implicated in EAMC, and we also know that body position is altered by the buoyancy of a wetsuit. Sighting requires head-raising, which alters body posture and so does swimming around buoys (and over other athletes). All of these movements differ from what you typically do in training. The solution begins with spending time training in cold open water with your wetsuit on, practicing sighting deep water, starts and turns, and swimming over your friends. But that is only a start.

In the gym, work the hamstring and calf muscles in various positions. Do hamstring curls. You can do this on a weight machine or lying on your back on the floor with a Swiss ball (Photo 1). Put your feet on the ball, lift your hips and roll the ball toward you, keeping the hips raised. Challenge yourself by doing this one leg at a time. Calf raises may help, too (Photo 2).

Photo 1.
Hamstring curl with Swiss ball

Photo 2.
Calf raise

Photo 3.
Using a foam roller
on calf

You should also spend time massaging the muscles with a foam or stick roller (Photo 3), which will help break up scar tissue in the muscle fibers to promote healthy circulation and muscle function.

CARBOHYDRATES, NOT SALT

The role of electrolytes is losing ground as a cause of EAMC. In the same 2005 study, researchers concluded that even during an Ironman race, sodium supplementation was not necessary to preserve serum sodium concentrations (among athletes competing for about 12 hours). The Institute of Medicine's recommended daily adequate intake of sodium (1.5 g/65 mmol) seems sufficient for a healthy person without further need to supplement during athletic activity (5).

Cramping is linked to muscle fatigue so feed your muscles well. Eat before your workouts and continue to consume 200-300 calories per hour especially during long workouts. Refuel afterward with a snack within 20 minutes and a meal within two hours.

PRACTICE

It is helpful to practice how you will deal with a cramp if you get one during a race. If you ever have a cramp, it is immediately obvious how it needs to be stretched. When you are doing an open water session, stop and practice floating as you stretch and massage the various muscles that tend to cramp; your calf, hamstring and foot. Belly breathe and stay relaxed. This bit of practice will help you manage if you get a cramp on race day.

SEASICKNESS

"Seasickness is the major cause of dropping out of the swim..."

– Ironman World Championship Athlete Information Guide

The most important interaction between vision and the ear is this maintenance of visual fixation, and it is well demonstrated by a water polo player swimming while keeping his eye on the ball (9).

If triathletes could swim fast and far without ever putting their heads in the water, seasickness would be less of a problem. But triathletes want to swim as efficiently as possible, so the head should be down most of the time and lifted only when necessary for navigation. The up and down motion of the head disturbs one's ability to maintain a visual fixation. To make matters worse, swells create large and often unexpected vertical accelerations (known appropriately as "heave"). Poor visibility due to murky water, goggles and a crowd of thrashing swimmers make it hard to get a visual fix on anything. Add to that an anxious athlete who knows she is sensitive to motion, and the expectation of seasickness can become a self-fulfilling prophecy.

Everyone is sensitive to motion to some degree or another; even fish get seasick. One study even found that people with high levels of aerobic fitness are especially susceptible to motion sickness, possibly because their autonomic nervous systems tend to be more reactive (10). What makes a person more or less sensitive is also a question of personal physiology (11).

Motion sickness is significantly more common in women, especially during or immediately before menstruation each month (12, 13). Sometimes seasickness is caused by a diagnosable medical condition that affects the eyes, ears, or both. If you have real difficulty with this issue and the strategies outlined here don't help, consider having a medical check-up.

Motion sickness can be effectively prevented with the medications discussed later, but they all have side effects. It is one thing to take a seasickness pill and go lie down, but quite another to take a pill and go out and race a triathlon. So what can a seasick triathlete do aside from taking medication? One options is to experiment with the strategies in this chapter well before race day. Finding something that works will do wonders for your confidence.

QUICK FIXES

- **Wetsuit:** Wetsuits provide extra buoyancy, but that can also make you less stable in the water and will bob you up and down along with the swells. Swim often in your wetsuit to get used to this sensation. Swim where the water is bumpy for progressively longer periods to build your tolerance.

- **Look at the horizon:** Dr. Charles Yanofsky of Pennsylvania Neurology Associates notes, "Seasickness is generally felt to be due to sensory mismatches. For example, the local up and down bobbing in the water gives the illusion of background movement, whereas the vestibular system tries to keep the environment image still, even as we move, so waves can be nauseating. Thus it sometimes helps to (sic) focus on a distant object that seems not to move." For this reason, turning over to do backstroke may only make matters worse because you will be looking up into the sky without a fixation point. Look at the horizon instead.

- **Look at landmarks:** Finding a visual fix is precisely what you attempt to do when you lift your head and look for the buoy, only the buoy is usually impossible to see because of the glare and turmoil around you. Instead of sighting to the buoy, pick a distant and much larger object that doesn't move, such as a tall tree, building or other landmark. This will give you something solid to look at.

- **Watch your hands:** Looking into murky water is like swimming blind, especially when you can't tell if you are looking 5 feet away or 2 inches. If you look at your arms or hands underwater as you swim, you will have a visual point of reference.

- **Move less:** Vertical movement is particularly likely to make you dizzy and nauseous, so don't add to the motion of the swells by lifting your head all the time. Learn to sight more to the side when you take a breath, lift your head less often, more slowly, or not as high.

- **Keep your head high:** Swim with your head slightly higher than usual so that you don't have to lift it much to see the buoy. This position creates more drag, but you will have the benefit of the wetsuit to minimize leg sinking. With practice, you can swim proficiently with your forehead, eyes and nose out of the water for long distances. This allows you to focus on a landmark for an extended time, which may calm your nausea. Make sure you practice this though. You will quickly get a stiff neck if you aren't "in shape" for swimming in this position. This is not an ideal swim position, but it is better than throwing up.

- **Avoid fumes:** Stay away from the chase boats and jet skis on race day. The fumes from these engines are toxic, carrying high levels of CO_2 and sulfur dioxide, which are dangerous and nauseating (14, 15).

- **Belly breathe:** Belly breathing is an effective way to reduce nausea and prevent its onset. You can't do it as you swim unless you stop for a few minutes, but you can do it before the gun goes off to reduce nervousness and the possibility of motion sickness. Use belly breathing with an habituation program like the one described below to make it more effective (16).

- **Don't swallow water:** A bellyful of brackish or salty water will not help matters. Practice swimming in the pool without letting water into your mouth. Dr. Robert Laird, the chief physician of the Ironman World

Championships in Hawaii, said ingestion of too much salt water can cause nausea and vomiting, which could lead to not being able to take in liquids and eventually severe dehydration (17).

- **Earplugs:** Nausea can be brought on by dizziness, which in turn can be caused by cold water going deep into the ear. Your problem may be solved if you wear earplugs in the water. There are numerous brands available so try several. If you experience dizziness with other kinds of exertion, you may have what is known as "exertional dizziness" which may indicate a dysregulation of the autonomic nervous system or possibly a heart problem. Check with your doctor.

- **Ginger:** Ginger appears to delay the onset of nausea and reduce the severity of motion sickness symptoms, but the mechanism is unknown. Ingesting one or two grams in capsule form, taken with water, one hour before the nausea-inducing event has been shown to be effective in many (but not all) studies (18). There are contradictory studies as well, but there aren't any known side effects, so it is worth a try.

- **Bigger goggles:** Tiny goggles virtually eliminate peripheral visual input, making it harder for the brain to reconcile the images. Try goggles that offer a wider field of vision. Remember, the eyes provide crucial input to the balance centers, so the more you can see, the better.

- **Acupressure:** Acupressure at the "P6" location has had mixed results. The pressure point is three finger-widths above the distal wrist crease (closest to the hand), in the middle of the third finger. Elastic bands (Sea-Bands) have a small button that presses on this spot. These bands can be worn during a race. There have been two studies testing the efficacy of the P6 acupressure for motion sickness, and no benefit was seen. Yet, the product appears to prevent post-operative and chemotherapy-induced nausea (19, 20, 21).

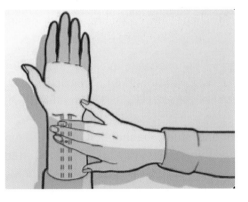

Figure 4. P6 location for acupressure.
Figure provided by Sea-Band

HABITUATION PROGRAMS

It is well accepted that repeated exposure to motion makes you less sensitive to it through the process of habituation. As unpleasant as it sounds, practicing making yourself (almost) seasick will probably help you.

Habituation is actually better than medication in reducing susceptibility to motion sickness (23). Habituation programs called "motion desensitization" are used extensively by the military because pilots can't be subjected to the side effects of medication. The success rate of these programs is over 85% (24).

Habituation programs are also prescribed by doctors and carried out by vestibular physical therapists is who call it "vestibular rehabilitation" or "balance training." These programs consist of a series of movements that progress from easy, non-disturbing movements to those that are more likely to cause dizziness and nausea. By practicing the movements, your body gets used to the sensations and becomes less sensitive to them. Here are some habituation-based options that might help you:

1. The discipline of tai chi is a form of habituation that is shown to improve balance (which may help with motion sickness) in participants (22).

2. The bumpiest part of the pool is right up against the wall, especially if there are no lane lines in place and there are other people swimming. Seek out this spot whenever you can to get plenty of jostling that will reduce your sensitivity.

3. A commercially available habituation program called the "Puma Method," was developed by a physician and pilot who wanted to find a way to deal with his own airsickness. The program is available on DVD or online.

In one study, habituation occurred more quickly when combined with belly breathing as soon as the subject started to feel ill (25). As few as four practice sessions may be enough to get your system habituated to the sensations that bring on nausea, so your response to nausea-inducing stimuli will be slower and less intense (26).

The information in this book will never replace what a doctor can do for you but you can create your own program and see if it helps (see Box 6). Incorporate the exercises into your training plan and swim sessions. I have personally suffered with vertigo, and this sort of program was a tremendous help.

HABITUATION GUIDELINES

Successful habituation programs have these characteristics (27):

1. High frequency of sessions with plenty of motion sickness-inducing exercises. The sessions must be done several times a week.
2. The exercises progress from easy, non-disturbing movements to more disturbing ones. Stop when you first feel ill, and allow recovery before starting again from the beginning.
3. Keep a positive mental attitude during the training.
4. Use belly breathing during the exercises.

When creating a program, master all of the movements with a single sense (vision) before adding another component (balance). Start at the beginning, going through the entire progression of each movement, each time you do a session. Over time, you will recover more quickly so the sessions will take less time, and eventually you will be able to get through all of the exercises without feeling nauseous.

Box 6. Sample homemade habituation program

1. Start in an upright position, seated in a chair. Turn your head slowly from side to side.
2. Next, move your head slowly, chin up then chin down.
3. Combine the head movements above, side to side, then up and down.
4. Bend at the waist and repeat 1-3 with your torso in a prone position (on your belly).
5. Repeat 1-3 while standing. This adds the element of balance.
6. Repeat 1-3 while standing on a Bosu ball (half of a Swiss Ball). This creates instability, which further challenges your balance.
7. It is a challenge to duplicate the sensation of swimming in rough water, so get creative about reenacting the vertical oscillation (up and down movement) that may be at the root of your sensitivity. Swinging and jumping on a trampoline may give you a similar sensation. "Anything you could do to simulate actual worst water conditions seems worthwhile. What about a wave pool? Another idea: read a book while running on a treadmill," adds Dr. Yanofsky.

MEDICATION

All of the motion sickness medications (28) have side effects, and there is evidence that taking them makes you more susceptible to motion sickness when the effect wears off (29). If you are considering their use, try them out well before race day. Medications work best when taken approximately one hour prior to your race. See your healthcare provider for more details on these treatments to decide which is best for you.

Scopolamine is a patch applied to the skin, which delivers medication slowly over three days and is highly effective. It must be used with caution in people with glaucoma and benign prostatic hypertrophy and can cause hallucinations, confusion, disorientation and memory disturbance. Other side effects include dry mouth and blurry vision, but there is less drowsiness than with other medications.

Antihistamines, such as Dramamine (generic name is dimenhydrinate) or Antivert (generic name is meclizine) are also effective, but a major side effect is drowsiness. There is a non-drowsy version of Dramamine, but try it before race day. It may still make you drowsy.

Medications for upset stomach, like Mylanta and Pepto Bismol, taken before the race may also be helpful and have fewer side effects.

© Bakke-Svensson/Ironman

CHAPTER 4
Worst Case Scenarios:
Triathlon Swimming Deaths

STATISTICS

Since 2002, at least 24 athletes have died during the swim leg of triathlons. A summary of each tragedy appears in Appendix D. Dr. Kevin Harris and his colleagues at the Minneapolis Heart Institute have analyzed 13 deaths that occurred between January 2006 and September 2008 to determine the statistical risk of death in triathlons.

Harris concluded that the risk of death per participation (not per athlete) in USAT sanctioned triathlons during that time period was 1.5 per 100,000 (1). That rate is much higher than for open water swimming events, which is only .12 in 100,000 (2).

What makes triathlon swimming so lethal? The Harris study was a good first step, but there are plenty of variables that have not been closely scrutinized in part because the information is not available. Autopsies were not done on every victim and some of the families have been silent toward the press. The autopsies that have been done have been generic, rather than investigatory.

Research is needed to determine which, if any, components of triathlon swimming put humans over the edge. The puzzle is far from solved. The following is a summary of some facts from the 24 deaths:

Race distance: Eight races were 70.3-distance or longer, six were Olympic distance, and 10 were sprints.

Age and gender of victims: Age ranged from 28-66 years old, spread roughly equally by generation starting at age 30. There were 21 men and three women.

Total race participation: In the Harris study, more people died in races with more than 300 participants than in smaller races. Race participation was not analyzed for the others.

The size of the race is not necessarily a reflection of crowding. There is not much difference between being surrounded by 20 athletes, 200 or 2,000 in terms of your immediate area. There are lots of bodies and splashing in all cases. The difference might be that in larger races the chaos *lasts longer* because there is less room to spread out after the first few minutes.

In some cases, the athlete succumbed almost immediately, in the thick of the crowd. Others lost consciousness late in the swim, when the crowd had thinned considerably. In one case, the athlete was one of the last two swimmers in the water so it could not have been crowded at that point, no matter how many athletes participated in the race.

Location: The deaths occurred at various places along the course. Some athletes succumbed in the first five minutes of the start, and others were in sight of the finish line. Relatively few were in the middle of the swim course.

Experience: The experience level of the athletes is not known in every case. Victims included at least 10 first-timers, several multiple-Ironman finishers, collegiate swimmers and seasoned triathletes.

WHY DO TRIATHLETES DIE DURING THE SWIM?

Sudden death can occur for various reasons. Statistically speaking, 95% of the deaths that occur suddenly are due to cardiovascular collapse.

Every part of a triathlon challenges the heart, but why do things go wrong in *the swim*? Below are several factors that set the swim apart from the other disciplines.

FACTOR ONE: HIGH ENERGY CHAOS

If you ask a triathlete what is hard about triathlon races, he will likely say that the physically hardest part is the run, but the most stressful part is the swim. The mayhem generated by hundreds of wetsuited athletes attempting to race in cold water en masse is about the most stressful thing one could do.

Athletes with a weakness in their cardiovascular systems are at a much higher risk of something going wrong. It is important to realize that some of the victims had a cardiac issue that they may not have known about. Figuring out whether you are one of those athletes is the best way to prevent a disaster. Chapter 5 discusses in detail the heart conditions you should be aware of and what you can do to evaluate your risk and assure that your heart is healthy as you train and race.

FACTOR TWO: UNCONSCIOUSNESS LEADS TO DROWNING

Sudden fainting may be the first sign of a heart problem, and if it happens in the water, you go under and drown. Events that are survivable on land are deadly in the water. Even a dizzy spell can become a life and death struggle if you don't know where the water's surface is.

The Harris study did not look at the number and nature of medical emergencies during the run and the bike. Athletes may get into the same kind of trouble, but because they are on land, they survive. We can't conclude that the swim is more *dangerous* than the other disciplines, only that, in races, it is more deadly.

FACTOR THREE:
THE WETSUIT QUESTION

Internet forums are replete with accounts of wetsuit-enhanced panic, claustrophobia, and difficulty breathing. Sometimes an athlete will even tear his wetsuit off mid-swim to be free of it. The physiological component does not appear to have been studied much beyond its influence on speed and energy expenditure. The interplay of the psychological and the physiological impacts of swimming in a wetsuit is an area ripe for study.

Triathletes are unique in the way they use wetsuits. They (and some open water swimmers) are the only people who wear wetsuits and race at high intensity for prolonged periods. Contrast this with SCUBA divers who make a point of moving little and slowly to conserve oxygen, or surfers who are mostly out of the water paddling in short bursts to catch a wave.

The wetsuit provides a barrier between the skin and the water. This influences the nervous system. It keeps cold water off the skin, but does it also modify important feedback?

Moreover, the wetsuit also compresses the body. The first thing a newbie says when they put on a wetsuit is, "Is it supposed to be this tight?" With all of the hype about the benefit of compression clothing as a recovery aid, no one appears to have studied the effect of varying levels of wetsuit compression on central and local vascular control during exertion. The compression decreased the compliance of the blood vessels. The resulting change in pulse propagation affects the action of baroreceptors, and thereby modifies heart dynamics.

Wetsuit compression may also stimulate the vagus nerve, which runs deep in the neck. Granted, a wetsuit would have to be exceptionally tight at just the right spot, but stimulation of this nerve can cause heart arrhythmias (3).

There is probably considerable variation in the amount of compression based upon styling, sizing, materials and manufacturer. Athletes also come in all shapes and sizes so some wetsuits may be tighter than others. Greater compression of the muscles and blood vessels in an athlete with large, developed legs may be a factor. Leg development may be an important difference between triathletes and open water swimmers.

Wetsuits clearly provide benefits for the great majority of triathletes. The question is how it impacts athletes who are, for one reason or another, *at risk*.

FACTOR FOUR:
WATER DELAYS DEFIBRILLATION

It is hard to notice a swimmer in distress when he is one among hundreds. Once spotted, it is difficult to reach a victim through the crowd. A recent Ironman event had 80 lifeguards and spotters in kayaks, 28 on paddle boards, 18 in powerboats, six spotting from shore and six on jet skis. There were also two boats and three dive teams. One has to wonder how many lifeguards and spotters are enough to ensure that rescue is quick enough to save a life.

There are certainly ways to make the swim safer, like sending swimmers off in groups of 10 with an escort, doing time trial type starts to eliminate large packs of swimmers, or requiring swimmers to wear a streamlined inflatable safety belt. However, all of these measures would interfere with the event in one way or another.
It would be relatively easy to put all the first timers in a "newbie" wave that has additional boats equipped with AEDs, but the victims have not always been first timers nor weak swimmers.

When someone suffers a cardiovascular collapse, survival is the exception, not the rule. According to the American Red Cross, sudden cardiac arrest (SCA) is one of the leading causes of death in the United States. It strikes over 300,000 people each year, of which about five percent survive; that's one of every 20.

The Red Cross has defined four critical steps, called the Cardiac Chain of Survival, for the treatment of SCA:

1. Early access to care (i.e., calling 911 or another emergency number),
2. Early cardiopulmonary resuscitation (CPR),
3. Early defibrillation, and
4. Early institution of advanced cardiac life support.

A break in any of the links in the chain can compromise the victim's chance for survival. Four of the victims disappeared underwater and were not recovered for minutes or even hours, but most of the victims were rescued quickly and CPR initiated shortly thereafter. The problem seems to be access to early defibrillation, which is recognized as *the most critical step in restoring cardiac rhythm*.

Defibrillation must be done within four minutes of losing consciousness. Every minute a victim is unconscious translates to approximately a 10% decrease in the likelihood of resuscitation. After 10 minutes, very few resuscitation attempts are successful (4).

Automatic External Defibrillators (AEDs) are widely used by rescue personnel, but they have limitations in a water environment. The AED delivers an electric shock to the victim, which will help bring his heart out of fibrillation, back into a productive rhythm. For obvious reasons, it cannot be used when either the victim or rescuer is in a puddle of water. Extra time is needed to make the area dry or to move the victim to a dry area. Time is in short supply for an unconscious swimmer.

It is hard to imagine a scenario in which a victim could possibly be identified *and* rescued *and* defibrillated *all within four minutes*. Short of collapsing on land and in front of an ambulance, there is little hope of survival in such a scenario.

FACTOR FIVE:
ATHLETES UNDERESTIMATE INJURY SYMPTOMS

It has been said that the standard of injury and awareness of it to which a triathlete aspires on race day is getting a deep cut in his foot at the swim exit and not knowing about it until he notices his bloody shoes after the finish line. Athletes often ignore or minimize injury symptoms, and they take pride in the ability to block out pain and discomfort. Separating training-related pain from signals of danger is one of the more difficult tasks an athlete has. "In the worst case (which is very rare), you die because something serious hits you and you don't know what it is but you keep on going" (5).

LEARNING FROM TRAGEDY

People die every day. The risk of dying during a triathlon swim is very small and the facts tell us that most of these athletes died because of something that was already wrong with them, but we can still learn from their deaths. Everything in this book is designed to make triathlon swimming safer and easier.

DON'T IGNORE EARLY CARDIAC SYMPTOMS

Signs of heart trouble can begin months or years before a fatal event. Certain heart conditions don't become symptomatic until later in life. The intense training that brings exceptional fitness may also trigger problematic cardiac changes in susceptible athletes.

Having years of symptom-free training does not mean a triathlete is free from undiagnosed conditions that can cause serious problems. It is terrifying to think that the first symptom of heart trouble could be death. This can be prevented in large measure by being properly screened on an annual basis.

Triathletes should learn about the symptoms of heart trouble so they can recognize them if they occur. They can occur at any time, not only during training sessions. Indeed, many symptoms are more likely to appear at rest, and they can come and go with varying intensity.

Heart arrhythmias can originate in different ways, and depending on the type, they can be deadly. Some of them start with symptoms that begin after dinner, at bedtime or early in the morning. Some symptoms can occur while swimming, so consider yourself lucky if you experience them on land.

They include:
- Palpitations (which you may not be able to distinguish from exertion while swimming)
- Dizziness (which can also be caused by cold water in the ears)
- Fainting (which causes drowning)

Coronary artery disease is another problem. The symptoms are more likely to appear during exertion, but they can also come at any time:
- Discomfort in your chest. You may feel a pressure or weight in your chest with activity or when breathing in cold air.

- Heaviness, pressure, aching, burning, fullness, squeezing in the chest shoulders, arms, neck, throat, jaw or back
- Palpitations (irregular heartbeats, skipped beats or a "flip-flop" feeling in your chest)
- Weakness or dizziness
- Sweating unrelated to exertion
- Fullness, indigestion, or choking feeling (may feel like heartburn)
- Nausea or vomiting
- Extreme weakness, anxiety
- Rapid or irregular heartbeats
- Feeling light-headed
- Fainting
- Shortness of breath and/or difficulty catching your breath. You may notice this most when you are active (doing your normal daily activities) or when you lie down flat in bed

DON'T IGNORE RACE DAY SYMPTOMS

Symptoms on race day can be attributed to multiple causes like anxiety, exertion or fatigue. Everyone who races feels a minor version of some of the symptoms listed above. Swimming is a unique physiological experience combining cold water, exertion and stress. It can be exceptionally difficult to tell the difference between your normal response and a troublesome one, especially in the early stages and/or if you are a nervous swimmer.

The eyewitness accounts of the triathlon deaths (Appendix D) indicate that at least eight of the 24 victims quickly and obviously signaled for help. They knew they were in trouble.

Interestingly, half a dozen other victims showed signs of difficulty but did not want to be rescued even when approached by lifeguards. They rested on kayaks, rolled onto their backs and, in some cases, even had ongoing conversations with lifeguards before suddenly becoming unconscious. Respiratory distress may have been the first and most prominent symptom. Stopping and resting was not typical for most of these swimmers, but they must have felt that they could overcome their symptoms with rest. It seems that they did not realize their symptoms were life-threatening until it was too late.

Respiratory difficulty is the first symptom of swimming induced pulmonary edema (SIPE), which has been documented in 1.4% of triathletes responding to an online survey. The behavior of the victims described above is what one would expect in swimmers suffering an episode of SIPE.

You should take any unusual difficulty with the swim seriously. For a new triathlete, it can be difficult to tell the difference between race day jitters and something more sinister. If you feel something that makes you want to repeatedly stop and rest, it's safest to get out of the water.

CHAPTER 5
Don't Ignore Your Heart

Most triathletes do not realize that they may be at risk for certain heart problems in spite of and because of their exceptional fitness.

The last thing you need on race day is fear that you will drop dead. Athletes in many sports are forced to retire due to heart conditions, and professional triathletes are no exception. Ultra Man David Goggins discovered that he had an atrial septal defect that limited blood flow in his heart output. Torbjorn Sindballe retired because of a dangerous heart valve abnormality and Ironman Champions Greg Welch and Emma Carney both suffered arrhythmias that ended their careers.

More than half of the triathlon swim fatalities are attributed to heart problems, including heart attacks, atherosclerotic disease, hypertensive cardiovascular disease, and cardiomyopathy (enlarged heart). Arrhythmias are another kind of problem. They involve electrical disturbances, and when they are fatal, they are difficult to diagnose because they do not leave clues as to their occurrence. It is possible that some of the athletes died because of arrhythmias.

A dangerous heart condition may not be on your list of Fear Factors, but maybe it should be.

ENDURANCE ATHLETES ARE AT RISK

Endurance athletes are up to five times more likely to suffer atrial fibrillation (AF) than the sedentary population (1). AF is a rapid and irregular contraction of the top chambers of the heart that causes the heart to beat irregularly.

Symptoms can appear during the athlete's competitive career or after they have stopped training and competing. Even after treatment with medication or surgery, endurance athletes have a higher incidence of recurrence of AF than the normal population (2).

AF can go on for years without causing problems, but it increases the risk of stroke by a factor of five to seven (3). It also decreases the heart's pumping ability by 20-25% and causes undue wear of heart muscles if it involves a chronic excessive heart rate. The risk of AF increases with age, especially after age 60. It affects one in every 10 persons aged 80 years or older, but some endurance athletes get symptoms much earlier.

The average athlete with AF is a middle-aged man (men outnumber women 4:1), between 40 and 50 years old, who has practiced regular endurance exercise since he was young and has never stopped completely. Training is his favorite leisure time activity, and he is psychologically very dependent on it. AF episodes are usually intermittent, occasional and self-limited, meaning the heart returns to a normal rhythm on its own. Episodes tend to become more frequent and prolonged over the years. Eventually they become persistent, becoming permanent in up to 17% of the affected individuals (4, 5).

AF episodes typically occur at night or after meals, and alcohol can be a precipitating factor. Episodes almost never occur during exercise. This makes the athlete reluctant to accept a relationship between the arrhythmia and training, especially since his physical condition is usually excellent (5).

The underlying mechanism of AF in endurance athletes is unknown, although structural atrial changes are probably part of it. There may also be a relationship between accumulated hours of practice (1500 hours of life-time exercise or more) and AF risk, but those numbers should be viewed with caution. A study of marathon runners showed that increased left atrial size, not hours of practice, was the greatest predictor of atrial fibrillation later in life (6).

The possibility of developing heart problems later in life *because* of your exceptional fitness is a hard pill to swallow. But don't hang up your running shoes just yet. AF doesn't occur in *all* endurance athletes. It is mostly connected to a small number of the athletes who develop athlete's heart — a cluster of changes that include enlargement of the heart chambers in response to exercise. Regular echocardiograms will indicate changes in heart structure, and if it occurs, you should discuss it with your doctor and be aware of the risk factors for developing problems later on.

IS ATHLETE'S HEART DANGEROUS?

Athlete's heart has traditionally been considered a harmless, temporary training adaptation. Changes occur in about half of athletes following 2-3 months of training (> 3 hours per week). Women show less cardiac change than men, even when controlled for age, body size and training intensity. The main changes are enlarged chamber volume, increased cardiac mass and a lower resting heart rate. These changes are the most dramatic in cyclists and rowers (7).

When training volume and intensity are reduced, the changes begin to reverse themselves. In most cases, the heart returns to normal dimensions after a few months away from training. But sometimes the changes remain for 30 years (8, 9). These cases lead researchers to consider whether the development of athlete's heart can bring about harmful, permanent changes (10).

An athlete who develops athlete's heart when he already has an inherited cardiac abnormality is at a much higher risk for fatal arrhythmias (11).

Echocardiograms can usually distinguish athlete's heart from enlargement due to other factors, but the distinction is not always clear. Of course, cardiac enlargement falls on a continuum from harmless to serious (10). The type of athletic training has a major influence on left ventricle dimension, so it is important that an evaluation includes details of your training regimen. Exercise testing is sometimes used to evaluate peak oxygen consumption, which helps to distinguish athlete's heart from inherited forms of cardiomyopathy (12).

HEART CONDITIONS LINKED TO SUDDEN CARDIAC DEATH

Sudden cardiac death (SCD) is abrupt, unexpected (meaning the victim didn't know he had a heart problem) and quick, occurring within minutes after the first symptoms appear. The most common cause of SCD is coronary artery disease, but there are other abnormalities that can cause sudden death. Luckily, nearly all of these abnormalities can be discovered before they kill. Therefore, it is imperative that you follow the preventative strategies at the end of this chapter.

OVER 35? LOOK FOR CORONARY ARTERY DISEASE

Sudden cardiac death in athletes over 35 is usually due to coronary artery disease, which restricts blood flow to the heart muscle. The arteries may be narrowed to the point that blood flow to part of the heart muscle is blocked or severely limited. Sometimes instead of narrow arteries, there is buildup of fatty material in the artery walls that cause trouble when it dislodges (often from stress hormones like adrenaline) and blocks blood flow to the heart muscle. You can evaluate your own level of risk for coronary artery disease in Appendix B.

Coronary artery disease sometimes produces symptoms only upon exertion, so a physical examination or ECG taken while a patient is at rest may not be sufficient for diagnosis. A person with symptoms of this disorder should have an ECG that is taken while he is exercising on a treadmill (stress test). A stress test is often used along with nuclear perfusion (injection of dye) to see blockages in coronary arteries.

CHECK FOR STRUCTURAL ABNORMALITIES

Sometimes abnormalities in the structure of the heart predispose it to arrhythmias. Arrhythmias are abnormalities in the heartbeat. Sometimes they are harmless; sometimes they are deadly. Severity depends upon where in the heart the arrhythmia occurs (which chamber) and how much it impairs the ability of the heart to pump blood. When an arrhythmia occurs in the ventricles, circulation can stop entirely, resulting in death. An arrhythmia in the atria is usually less serious.

The most common abnormality is an enlarged heart (cardiomyopathy), which can be inherited, acquired through illness or developed as an adaptation to training (athlete's heart).

CHECK FOR INHERITED ABNORMALITIES

Sudden cardiac death in athletes under age 35 is usually due to inherited abnormalities that involve enlargement of the ventricles. Two dangerous conditions in this category are hypertrophic cardiomyopathy (HCM) and arrythmogenic right ventricular cardiopathy (ARVC). People with these conditions should not participate in competitive sports. Although these are inherited conditions, the symptoms may not appear until later in life so it is important to have a screening before you get serious about training, no matter what your age.

ILLNESS CAN INCREASE RISK

Few people realize that fatigue or flu-like symptoms increase the risk of cardiac arrhythmias. Inflammation of the heart muscle known as myocarditis, is one of the more common and serious complications of an infection. It can occur without obvious symptoms, and it can be deadly. Myocarditis causes sudden cardiac death in 5-22% of athletes under age 35 (13). Parvovirus B19 and human herpes virus 6 are the most important pathogens leading to the condition.

Inflammation can scar the heart muscle and make it more susceptible to deadly arrhythmias (14). A virus may bring no symptoms but result in an abnormal ECG. Others may experience an aching feeling in the chest, or cold or flu-like symptoms. Serious cases may cause shortness of breath, leg swelling, fever, chest pain or abnormally fast, slow or irregular heartbeats and fainting (15).

Dr. Mark Timmerman, a four-time Ironman participant who practices family and sports medicine, tells triathletes that if they're not feeling well, they shouldn't push it, and they shouldn't swim in cold water if they are sick. "It's hard for someone if they've trained a lot to not do an event. You put in all that time and all that sacrifice, and if you have a fever you really shouldn't compete. It's really tough on your heart," he says (16).

LONG QT AND SWIMMING

There are a multitude of abnormalities that influence the timing and spread of electrical impulses through the heart. One of the more common genetic conditions appearing in 2.5% of the population is known as long QT syndrome. The long QT syndrome (LQTS) is characterized by prolongation of the recharging phase of the heart after it beats. One type of LQTS seems particularly sensitive to swimming. Statistically, individuals with this type of LQTS are 10 times more likely to suffer a particular type of fatal arrhythmia while swimming, compared with other types (17).

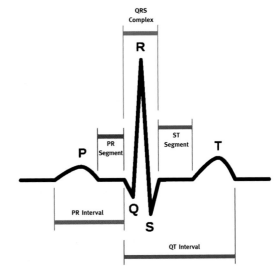

Figure 5. Some important time intervals on an ECG

People with LQTS are at risk for a certain arrhythmia that can cause fainting, cardiac arrest, or sudden death, usually in young, otherwise healthy individuals (18). In most cases, symptoms will first appear in childhood.

PREVENTION

Lawrence L. Creswell, MD, is a heart surgeon and Associate Professor of Surgery at the University of Mississippi Medical Center. He is an avid triathlete and has a special interest in heart diseases in endurance athletes. Dr. Creswell has the following recommendations for triathletes:

Perhaps the most important strategy is for triathletes to be thoughtful about the possibility of having pre-existing heart disease. In addition, I recommend that all adult athletes have an ECG and echocardiogram (more expensive), at least on one occasion, to screen for any congenital heart disease and common heart rhythm abnormalities that may place them at increased risk for sudden death during athletic competition. A resting ECG done once can exclude inherited rhythm problems, such as long QT syndrome that predispose athletes to sudden death. It will also identify any permanent abnormal rhythm that might deserve attention.

An ECG done in the physician's office may be normal despite the presence of paroxysmal (intermittent) atrial arrhythmias that occur during exercise or early afterwards. These arrhythmias can sometimes be captured on a Holter monitor, an ECG that is made over a period of 24-72 hours.

For triathletes who are truly healthy (no medical problems), a baseline ECG and echocardiogram are probably sufficient when combined with an annual physical examination that focuses on the cardiovascular system .

Having regular screenings in accordance with these recommendations is important so you can be confident that you are swimming healthy.

CHAPTER 6
Breathe Easy

Breathing difficulties of any kind are alarming. This chapter describes some of the breathing-related problems that triathletes may encounter when swimming and what can be done about them.

HYPERVENTILATION

Hyperventilating will force you to slow down, but it probably (except in very rare cases) won't kill you.

When you become aware of your breathing for some reason, you may take an extra large breath in an effort to relax. This over-breathing uses your chest muscles to expand your rib cage. The extra muscle work feels like shortness of breath. The reduced carbon dioxide levels in the blood constrict the airways, which makes you wheeze. You realize you are wheezing and get even more anxious, which makes matters worse. The best way to deal with this is to resist the urge to fix the problem with more breathing; less will work better. If you get this feeling in the middle of the race, the belly breathing protocol of 12 breaths per minute won't work. Slow down a little and try breathing a little less often while focusing on how much your legs hurt instead of on your breathing. You may have to stop completely to calm yourself. Seek medical help if the symptoms don't resolve in a few minutes.

EXERCISE-INDUCED ASTHMA

Exercise is a common trigger of asthma attacks. When exercising, you breathe through your mouth. The air that hits your lungs is colder and drier than the warm, humid air that hits your lungs when you breathe through your nose. The temperature and moisture difference can trigger an attack.

The airways may swell and secrete large amounts of mucus, which can partially block the airways, making it more difficult exhale. The mucus should not be bloody or brown. If it is, it may be something different, like swimming induced pulmonary edema (SIPE), the symptoms of which are is described in the next section.

Symptoms of exercise-induced asthma usually begin about five to 20 minutes after beginning to exercise and peak five to 10 minutes afterward. Then they gradually diminish. Symptoms are typically gone within an hour, but they may last longer. Symptoms can include (1):

*   Coughing
*   Wheezing
*   Chest tightness
*   Chest pain
*   Prolonged shortness of breath
*   Difficulty exhaling
*   Extreme fatigue

Asthma cannot be cured, but it can be controlled by medication that is taken before exercise.

SWIMMING-INDUCED PULMONARY EDEMA

Charles C. Miller, III, PhD is an epidemiologist who works primarily in cardiovascular disease. He is Chair of the Department of Biomedical Sciences, Associate Dean for Research and Associate Dean for the Graduate School of Biomedical Sciences at the Texas Tech Paul L. Foster School of Medicine in El Paso, Texas. Dr. Miller had a SIPE episode in 2001 and kindly contributed his expertise to this section. He also wrote an article that appears in Appendix C. Dr. Miller is not related to the book's author.

Triathletes occasionally report breathing problems in the swim, which include shortness of breath that seems out of proportion to the work being done, and cough productive of copious amounts of pink, frothy, brown or blood-tinged sputum. This is known as swimming induced pulmonary edema (SIPE), and it is different than what is encountered in the elderly, in patients with heart disease, or in athletes on dry land. Dry land pulmonary edema requires immediate medical attention, while SIPE is usually (though not always) self-limiting.

Most people report SIPE within the first 15-20 minutes of a swim, though it can start later in very long events. A swimmer who experiences an unfamiliar shortness of breath and a productive cough should spit out what he or she is coughing up and get a look at it. You need to know if it's pink, frothy or bloody, so you can tell your doctor later.

SIPE is distinct from exercise-induced asthma (or any kind of asthma for that matter) in that asthma is characterized by wheezing, tightness in the airways, and an impaired ability to blow air out of the lungs. Sputum produced by asthma is not pink or bloody.

SIPE is estimated to occur in approximately 1.4% of triathletes (2), and appears to occur in generally healthy people. SIPE has also been reported in Navy SEALS, as well as in apnea (breath-holding) divers and SCUBA divers. It should be taken seriously but should not lead to panic. People with normal blood pressure who have never had an episode are at very low risk and should not be worried about it.

Symptoms usually resolve on their own once the person gets out of the water and calms down, although in some cases supplemental oxygen and diuretics may be administered. Athletes, and especially ultra-endurance athletes, are a hard-driven bunch, and many of them will want to get back in the game as soon as the episode resolves. In a sport that involves navigating a crowded bike course and a demanding run, this is not a good idea. SIPE should end the day's performance but not a triathlete's career.

Prevention strategies and the decision to continue competition afterward is a personal one that should be made in the context of advice from a competent physician. Don't be surprised if most personal physicians are not familiar with SIPE. A good consultation is most likely to be had with a sports-oriented cardiologist or family physician specializing in sport medicine.

Several follow-up studies in directly observed SIPE cases in military populations have not demonstrated any harm or lingering effects. Cardiac and pulmonary function tests return to normal within a few weeks.

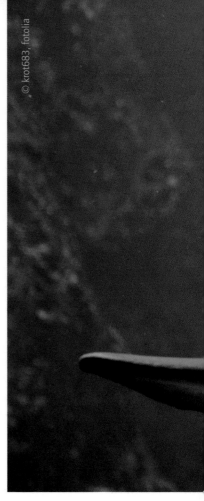

RISK FACTORS

Swimming induced pulmonary edema is believed to result from a "perfect storm" of various potential risk factors that affect pressure in lung structures and the ability of the body to regulate that pressure. These factors include: 1) water immersion; 2) exertion; 3) cold water; 4) over-hydration; 5) pulmonary capillary trauma; 6) neurohumoral abnormalities; 7) position in the water; 8) use of a tight wetsuit, 9) diastolic cardiac dysfunction; and 10) blood-thinning medications. The more technical aspects of SIPE are discussed in Appendix C.

PREVENTION

The most obvious preventative strategies are to avoid overhydration prior to the swim and to treat any underlying conditions such as high blood pressure or diabetes. Athletes who have had an episode of SIPE should discuss a prevention plan with their doctor.

CHAPTER 7
Don't Be Afraid of Sharks

"I feel sorry for it. That shark is going to have to wake up at 5:15 am every morning when my Timex starts beeping."

—Chuck Anderson, triathlete who lost his arm to a bull shark in June 2000(1)

The most dangerous sea creature on earth doesn't have teeth. Its victims rarely see it coming and when it gets them they suffer excruciating pain that can last for weeks. Scarring is horrific and permanent. It is instantly lethal to most sea life. If you are lucky, you will get to shore before going into cardiac arrest. This predator is so dangerous that swimmers don't go in the water when it is near. Beach nets don't stop it. Yet, it is so delicate it can be torn apart by a struggling shrimp. The box jellyfish lives in the seas of the tropic north and the east pacific. It is said to have caused 5,567 deaths since 1884 (2). That makes it much more lethal and much more common than sharks, yet there aren't many triathletes who would put this jellyfish on their list of Fear Factors. There is only one sea creature that seems to keep triathletes out of the ocean — sharks.

SHARKS AND TRIATHLETES

The Escape from Alcatraz Triathlon may call its venue "a major shark nursery," but there has never been a shark attack in the San Francisco Bay. Indeed, there has never been one at a triathlon.

Erich Ritter, PhD., is a professional applied shark-human interaction specialist. He has studied the body language of sharks, shark attacks and their causes and has challenged traditional notions of why sharks attack. Ritter is the head of the SharkSchool™, an institution that teaches divers, snorklers, rescue swimmers and others how to interact with sharks, what to look for when entering the water and how to feel safe among sharks. A former Ironman athlete himself, Ritter has spent his life studying shark behavior. He says it is very unlikely that a shark would be attracted to the chaos generated by hundreds of wetsuit-clad athletes scrambling through the sea.

Racing isn't the problem. Training is the problem.

Three triathletes have been attacked by sharks while training; one of whom died.

In June 2000, a pair of triathletes tangled with a shark in Gulf Shores, Alabama. Chuck Anderson, 44, lost his right arm above the elbow and Richard Watley. 55, was bitten on his right hip and right arm (1).

In April 2008, 66-year-old David Martin died from blood loss after a 16-foot great white bit him as he swam with eight other triathletes. It happened less than a mile from the Solana Beach Triathlon course in San Diego, California.

IMPORTANT SHARK FACTS:

1. People go into the sea to swim, surf, dive and play over 150 million times a year in the United States. One or two fatalities from per year is a miniscule number in comparison (3).

2. Being killed by a shark in any given year is about as likely as being killed by a coconut falling on your head, about 1 in 251,800,000 (4, 5).

3. Despite the terror it provokes, 70% of shark "attacks" involve minimal force and are not fatal. Says George Burgess, director of the International Shark Attack File in Gainesville, "every shark attack elicits the same reaction whether it's a nick or a very serious injury." (6)

4. Of the more than 460 shark species, only a few of them grow large enough to cause serious injuries to people. Most are much too small to do much damage.

5. "If people followed the guidelines (see Box 7), we could probably cut down shark attacks to half," says Burgess. "That change would be welcome, but won't do much to change a person's chances of being attacked because it goes from an infinitesimal chance (of being attacked) to half of an infinitesimal chance" (8).

YOU ARE NOT SHARK FOOD

If sharks were really interested in eating people, the beaches would be piled with chewed up surfboards, and no one would survive an attack. Attacks would be commonplace and fatal, with people disappearing in the ocean all the time. Humans are easy prey — they aren't very fast, they aren't very strong and they can't do much more than kick and thrash. They are much easier prey than pinnipeds (seals and sea lions). The reason there aren't more accidents is simply that sharks don't see humans as prey. The unknown is always potentially dangerous and, even for the shark, approaching a human harbors a certain risk. For a shark to approach or bite an unknown object is thus an exception and not the rule (6)

SHARKS KNOW THAT YOU ARE NOT A SEAL

Sharks have a highly sophisticated sensory system. They hear, smell and see, and they also have "electrosense," which enables them to sense weak electric fields emitted by some ocean life. They can smell 10 drops of tuna oil in a swimming pool and one drop of blood 1/3 of a mile away. A disturbance can thus draw sharks from some distance away, and they may come to investigate.

Sharks did not evolve with humans in their environment so they don't know what humans are. Sharks are at the top of the food chain, and since they have no natural predators, they are confident in nature (especially the large bull, tiger and great whites, which are more often involved in attacks). These species are also more curious than other species. Greater confidence and curiosity seems to go along with approaching unknown objects, like people, on rare occasions.

When they do, their senses send them signals that aren't quite right for food or anything else within the realm of their experience. Sharks approach objects made of all different materials, shapes and sizes. Ritter has experimented and found that a shark is no more likely to bite a floating object that resembles a pinniped than one that does not. If the object is moving away from the shark, a bite is more likely. The movement may stimulate chase behavior in the shark. When a shark is curious about an object in the water, it approaches slowly from behind or below. In contrast, a shark attacking prey zooms in at great speed, often jumping out of the water as it snaps it up. Sea lions are formidable biters themselves, so sharks rely on the element of surprise and come at these animals with everything they have to make quick work of them.

Shark accidents involving humans are not nearly as forceful as attacks on sea mammals, supporting the notion that these bites are more exploratory.

A shark probably bites to determine whether an unknown object is edible. The shark's mouth has receptors that evaluate whether something is a tasty, high-fat pinniped and thus food, or something else. Bony, lean humans aren't food, and sharks react accordingly by letting go and swimming away.

SHARKS ARE NOT ATTRACTED TO HUMAN BLOOD

Female triathletes may feel especially vulnerable to sharks during their menstrual cycle. But rest easy, for sharks are not thrown into a "feeding frenzy" by human blood.

Ritter says, "no two blood types are the same. ... The blood of every animal species has a specific, individual composition consisting of plasma proteins, inorganic (sic.) ions and salts, organic nutrients and nitrogen waste products, to name just a few. Research shows that sharks possess extremely sensitive smelling organs, which developed over millions of years and make them react to proteins rather than sugar. But even with its highly specialized sense of smell, the shark can only identify animals which he knows

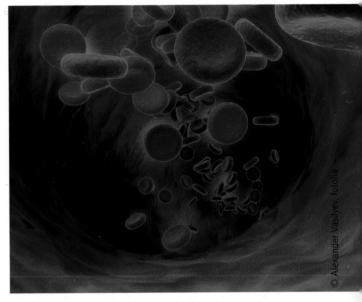

© Alexander Vasilyev, fotolia

based on their blood composition. Certain elements in the blood may remind him of familiar organisms and thus trigger an approach maneuver. Still, the shark knows that the blood which he smells is not completely familiar to him and will near the object very cautiously" (6).

"My advice," asks Burgess, "Don't worry about it. Lots of women safely dive while menstruating. Although we haven't got solid scientific data on the subject, so far we haven't seen any obvious pattern of increased attacks" (8).

WHERE THE SHARKS ARE

Detailed statistics about shark accidents worldwide are available at http://www.flmnh.ufl.edu/fish/Sharks/Statistics/statistics.htm.

Below is a list of the 10 most common locations for shark accidents (10):

1. Volusia County, Florida — New Smyrna Beach is the "Shark Attack Capitol of the World." It has more shark incidents per square mile than any beach in the world, and if you've been swimming there, you've probably been within 10 feet (3 meters) of a shark.
2. South Africa — Dyer Island, near Cape Town, has earned the nickname "Shark Alley" for the many species of sharks in the water, including great whites. Kosi Bay is full of bull sharks.
3. New South Wales, Australia
4. Hawaii — Oahu and Maui
5. Queensland, Australia
6. Brevard County, Florida
7. Brazil — Recife is a shark haven featuring a shark breeding estuary, feeding grounds, and a slaughterhouse, which disposes of blood in nearby tributaries. One in three shark accidents in Recife are fatal.
8. California — Two popular beaches, Bolinas and Stinson, are in the "Red Triangle" area from Bodega Bay, north of San Francisco, to Ano Nuevo Island near Santa Cruz with the corner of the triangle being the Farallon Islands. This is the world's leading site of great white shark attacks on humans. The sharks are attracted by the large population of seals in the area.
9. South Carolina — The majority of attacks have occurred in Horry County, home to popular Myrtle Beach.
10. Papua New Guinea

HOW TO PREVENT AN ACCIDENT

Preventing a shark accident starts long before you get into the water. Awareness of your surroundings and of what sharks are interested in is the first step. No matter where you are, it is important to take a look around you before you go charging into the water. These recommendations are based upon information from the Shark Research Institute, Inc., (6) (see Box 7).

We are used to ignoring signs, but if a shark has been spotted in a particular area, most likely a warning sign will be posted. Don't forget to read the signs at the beach. Sharks are more likely to feed at dawn, dusk and in the dark, so don't go swimming at those times. Murky water makes it more difficult for sharks to accurately evaluate whether or not you are a food source, especially when you are surrounded by fish, so avoid murky water.

NOTICE LOCAL WILDLIFE

Consider that if sharks are in the area, they are chasing fish and sea lions. If you see bait jumping or "running" on the surface of the water, it is because they are being pursued by a predator. If sea birds have gathered and are diving into the water, they are after fish that are on the surface. Why are they there? A beached sea lion may have been driven out of the water. Dolphins are known to cluster together to protect themselves from sharks.

Once you are in the water, you may be delighted to see a large school of fish gathering around you. It may mean you are exceptionally attractive to fish or it could be that the fish are using

Box 7: Shark Do's and Dont's (9)

Don't swim near food sources:
- Sea lion rookeries
- Fishing boats
- Fishing piers or jetties
- River mouths
- Sandbars
- Drop offs where the water becomes suddenly much deeper
- Spear fishermen with catch
- Where bait fish are jumping out of the water.

Don't swim at dawn, dusk or in the dark.

Don't swim near shelters:
- Pods of dolphin
- If you are suddenly surrounded by fish, leave the water
- Sharks are drawn to shelter for their prey so avoid piers, jetties, and reefs

Don't swim in murky water.

Swim near lifeguards.

Swim with a buddy or two.

Don't call attention to yourself in the water with excessive splashing.

Don't swim with dogs or horses because their erratic splashing may attract predators.

Don't wear high contrast clothing or shiny objects.

Swim with goggles, and open your eyes underwater.

you as a hiding place because there are sharks in the area. Leave the water if fish start to cluster around you. Sharks are also more likely to go after solitary prey, so don't swim alone.

In order to see what is going on around you, you have to have your eyes open. Sounds simple, but many triathletes don't open their eyes under water because they are afraid of what they might see. Later I will tell about the things you can do to discourage a shark while it is still some distance away, but you have to see it first.

AVOID SHELTERS

Sharks are known to hang around reefs, shipwrecks, piers and jetties. These structures provide the shark with cover as they stalk prey, as well as being havens for the wildlife sharks feed upon. If you want to avoid sharks, avoid these places.

Sharks seem to have a notion of "personal space" and will respond when you enter their "outer circle." The size of the circle varies by species. Typically a shark will swim away to keep you at a preferred distance, but if you are swimming near a shelter, you may inadvertently box the shark into a space from which it cannot readily escape. This may trigger defensive behavior.

WHAT TO DO IF YOU SEE A SHARK

There are plenty of people who want to swim with sharks. Divers routinely see them and live to tell about it. Indeed, look at some scuba diving websites, and you will find all sorts of first-hand accounts about how wonderful swimming with sharks can be. If you were a diver, you may well think seeing a shark is the grandest thing ever. The point is, seeing a shark does not mean you are going to die. A shark encounter is not the same as a shark attack.

Your actions can influence what a shark does. Dr. Ritter has spent many hours swimming with sharks and teaching others to do it safely.

Here is his advice:
"If the shark gets within two body lengths, move towards it. Swimming away from the shark can provoke his instinct to chase. Swimming towards the shark will not trigger him into attacking. Instead, he will swim away or at least seek a greater

distance (the so-called outer circle). It is important to always keep an eye on the shark. Many times, divers (perhaps out of fear) simply look away, hoping somewhat naively that the shark did not see them. But he has! Sharks orient themselves to our bodies and recognize our head-oriented coordination, even when they actually do not "know" what a human is. The diver MUST signal to the shark that he has seen him, and the best way to do this is to swim towards him! Admittedly, this requires strong nerves" (6).

Photo 4. The recommended sculling position you should use if a shark comes near.
Photo provided by Eric Ritter

'If a shark gets so close that you feel you have to do something, push it away, but don't do anything violent. If a shark grabs you, try to grab or poke the gills which are very sensitive. The eyes are sensitive as well but they are too small a target."

I asked Ritter specifically what a triathlete should do if he/she sees a shark, and he said, "Go into a vertical position, scull with the arms and turn with the shark (so he sees that you are aware of him (sic.)." Photo 4 illustrates the position.

If a shark bites you, blood loss is the biggest danger. Stop the bleeding as well as you can by applying direct pressure to the wound. Swim away quietly but keep your eye on the shark, even if you have to swim backwards.

KEEPING SHARKS AWAY

NETS

In Australia, popular beaches are surrounded by nets designed to catch sharks more than 6.6 feet (2 meters) in length and drum lines, baited hooks meant to catch sharks. Keeping sharks away from swimmers is standard protocol for triathlon race directors. This protocol utilizes a combination of helicopter patrols, boats in the water and observation towers staffed by lifeguards.

However, the nets bring controversy from environmentalists who are concerned the nets may kill sharks and other sea animals. These debates are hot topics in New South Wales, and especially near Sydney and Queensland. In 2005, in response to outcry about a baby humpback whale killed in the nets, the Queensland government released figures relating to the nets' success. In one year, 630 sharks were caught; 298 of those were greater than 6.6 feet (2 meters), including a 17-foot (5.2-meter) tiger shark. The nets and drum lines have been effective, but the environmentalists favor building caged areas around the swimmers. Technology may soon come to the rescue providing alternative measures to keep swimmers safe.

REPELLANTS

CHEMICAL REPELLANTS

Scientists have battled for years to find an effective way to repel sharks. The quest became more urgent during World War II, when the U.S. Navy looked for a way to protect downed personnel forced to abandon ships in the ocean. The Shark Chaser, a life jacket filled with chemicals repulsive to sharks, proved ineffective (11). The search for a chemical repellent continues.

Testing on a sprayable repellant called SharkSkunker is underway. It is made from the foaming ingredient in shampoo, toothpaste and other household cleaners, which settles temporarily on the shark's gills and is unpleasant; it is touted as is eco-friendly and effective. It is carried in a large jug and when sprayed at sharks, it seems to repel them for 15-20 minutes. The product has not yet been rigorously tested.

There are natural repellants as well. A particular species of flatfish that lives in the Red Sea has pores that secrete a milky fluid that, among other things, repels sharks for up to 18 hours. John R. Williams, PhD, and Professor of Chemistry at Temple University, is working to synthesize and test new forms of the substance Pavoninin-4 to make it more active and a lot cheaper. Dr. Williams notes, "no one is going to pay $1,000 per swim to be shark free in a triathlon." They envision a time-release method of application.

ELECTRIC REPELLANTS

Electronic devices have been evolving for more than a decade. The early versions were bulky and could be carried only on scuba diving tanks like the ones used during the 2000 Sydney Summer Olympics. Divers wearing a device

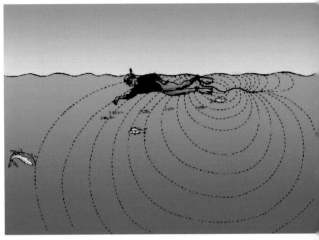

Photo 5. Swimmer wearing a Shark Shield Freedom 7 model for swimmers.
Photo used with permission of SharkShield.

Figure 6. Illustration of electrical shield produced by SharkShield. Used with permission.

called the SharkShield (a.k.a., SharkPod), swam beneath triathlon competitors to protect them from sharks. See Photo 5.

The SharkShield forms an unpleasant electrical current, which is detected by the shark's electricity sensors located on the shark's snout. The manufacturer suggests SharkShield is effective in shark repulsion over distances as long as 8 meters.

SharkShield is widely used by professional divers and fisherman who are in the water with sharks all day. A single fatality has called its effectiveness into question although it is unclear whether the device had been used correctly at the time (12). The obvious problem with Shark Shield is the antenna that drags a few feet behind a swimmer. For more information, go to their website, http://www.sharkshield.com.

ACOUSTIC REPELLANT

The Sharkstopper is an acoustic device that uses, in part, recorded sounds of killer whales, a natural enemy of sharks. Well-known shark expert, A. Peter Klimley was consulted on the viability of the product. He freely admitted that the theory was sound but he remains skeptical.

George H. Burgess said the device is based on well-known biological facts and engineers at the University of Florida are working to develop a similar electric fence that would guard beaches where sharks encountering humans is a major concern.

"This is a device for those who are working regularly in an area where there is a demonstrated presence of dangerous sharks and for those who are paranoid about sharks and will do anything to minimize the risk," said developer Brian Wynne. The

Photo 6. Sharkstopper device worn on the ankle like a timing chip. Photo used with permission.

swimmer-sized model straps around the ankle and is about the size of a GPS unit. See Photo 6. It will retail for about $150, and it is planned for release to the public in 2011 (12).

FINDING COURAGE

Chuck Anderson went on to do 17 more triathlons, some in the ocean, after his accident. The eight triathletes swimming with Dave Martin when he died are still swimming in the ocean, too. So are Dave's son and grandchildren.

"I did lots of research about sharks. I learned that what happened to Dave is extremely unusual. Much less likely than anything you can imagine. It is 80 times more likely that you will get struck by lightning and much more likely that you will win the lottery," says Ken Flagg, one of the athletes who swam with Dave that day. "I took about a week to get back in the ocean, and I have made some changes to my routine, but I acknowledge that the changes I have made are based more on superstition and bad memories than facts. I still swim in the ocean several days each week."

I asked Ken what worries beginner triathletes, and he said they were afraid to swim in the ocean because of sharks. He replied, *"Many people have asked me this question. Many do not know what I went through. I tell them that it is not going to happen. Cars and bikes are much more dangerous. Most importantly, I encourage everyone to swim with a buddy. There are many things that can go wrong in the ocean, and it will almost certainly not have anything to do with a shark."*

Laurene Booth was only few feet from Dave when he was attacked. She felt compelled to get back into the ocean too, in part as a tribute to Dave and to show support for his son, Jim, and his kids who decided to take up triathlon in Dave's honor. As time passed, Laurene was able to refocus on the details of her upcoming races and renew her love for the sport.

The day after the accident, Dave's son Jim went into the water at Fletcher Cove to reclaim his connection with the ocean he so loved. The shark warning signs were still up.

Laurene, Ken and Jim all raced the Solana Beach Triathlon less than three months after the accident, with "Go Dave" written on their arms. In spite of the accident, the number of participants in the race was actually up from the previous year.

As we age, we realize more and more how dangerous life can be. At some point, caution starts to rob you of one pleasure after another until eventually you are resigned to a rocking chair. Triathletes resist mightily the notion of giving up and giving in. If you want to swim in the ocean, do it.

There are all sorts of ways to minimize triathlon-related risks by having a medical check-up, riding with a helmet, respecting traffic rules, etc. The risk of a shark attack need not be on the list of *true* risks.

FEARLESS SWIMMING STRATEGIES

1. Follow the Fearless Swimming Safety Rules (Tools 1-4) and the precautions set forth in this chapter.
2. Consider using a shark repellant.
3. Shark accidents are extremely rare, especially compared to auto accidents. Auto accidents are much more dangerous but, like shark accidents, they share the element of surprise (in many cases). Do people involved in auto accidents stop driving? Usually not. Do people who have never been in an accident stop driving because they are afraid of getting into an accident? Rarely. If you have the nerve to drive, you have the nerve to swim in the ocean.
4. Pretend a beginner triathlete has come to you expressing concern over sharks. What would you say to help?
5. Separate myth from fact; educate yourself. Remember that sharks are not really interested in you.
6. Create a desensitization plan to overcome your fear of swimming in the ocean. Focus on the Fearless Swimming Skills and master the art of calming yourself with belly breathing, developing the right mindset, and, if need be, overwriting bad memories (Tools 6, 14 and 15)
7. The few people involved in the shark incidents described here are still swimming in the ocean. *If they can do it, so can you.*

Special thanks to Eric Ritter, PhD, and triathletes Ken Flagg and Laurene Booth for providing the email interviews that contributed to this chapter.

Section 2:
Fearless Swimming Skills

"Skill and confidence are an unconquered army."
George Herbert (1593-1633)

THE FEARLESS SWIMMING SKILLS

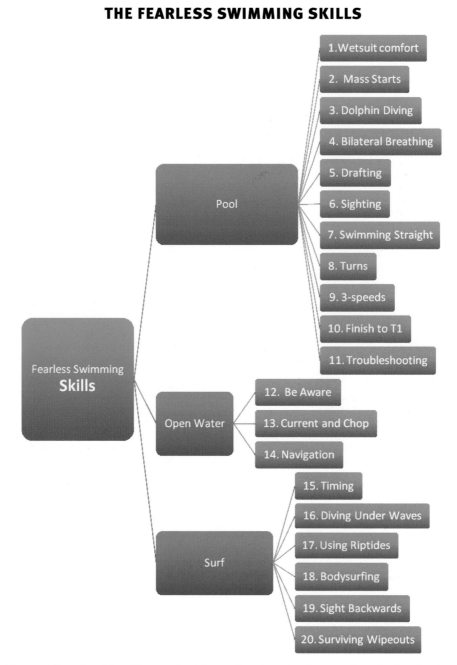

The number that identifies each skill on the chart is also used in the book where it is first discussed. The application of these skills is described in various contexts throughout Section 2.

© Bakke-Svensson/Ironman

CHAPTER 8
Love Your Wetsuit

SKILL #1: WETSUIT COMFORT

The warmth and buoyancy of wetsuits may theoretically attract weak swimmers to the sport of triathlon, but the reality is that the very thing that should give a beginner confidence may ultimately give him grief as recounted by this tri newbie:

"The horn went off. I lurched forward and plunged down into the water. There was a frenzy of arms and legs splashing about. I got out 50 yards or so when I realized things were not quite right. My breathing was very labored. I stopped, gasping for air, and felt this intense choking sensation. It was as if my wetsuit had come alive and begun strangling me and wrapping itself tighter and tighter around my chest. I was treading water and began to panic. My first instinct was to keep moving so I got my arms going again and thought that maybe I could relax and get in a groove. No such luck. The choking sensation intensified and, to make matters worse, I suddenly couldn't bring myself to submerge my face under the water. Complete mind block. By this time, I was in a full panic attack. Thoughts flashed through my mind like lightning bolts. *What if I have to pull out after only 50 yards? How embarrassing if I have to be rescued. Maybe triathlons aren't my cup of tea. What's the deal with this friggin' wetsuit?"* (1).

A fast wetsuit is no substitute for swim fitness and plenty of open water practice. Indeed, about the worst thing a newbie can do is to put on his wetsuit for the first time on race day.

Is wetsuit comfort really a fearless swimming skill? You bet it is. Nothing can ruin a swim faster than an uncomfortable wetsuit. Achieving comfort requires:

- A wetsuit that is the right size,
- A wetsuit that is adjusted properly so it fits you well, and
- Plenty of open water practice swimming in the wetsuit.

BUY THE RIGHT ONE

All wetsuits are not created equal. Triathlon wetsuits are designed for the motion of continuous swimming. Trying to swim in a surfing or diving wetsuit is miserable. Surfing wetsuits are meant for short bursts of paddling and sitting or standing on your board. Diving wetsuits are designed for warmth as you move in slow motion underwater. If you wear the wrong kind of wetsuit, you will be cold, immobile and claustrophobic, not to mention the serious chaffing that can occur. Wear a triathlon wetsuit or don't wear a wetsuit at all.

Many store and online sources allow you to rent a wetsuit for race day and then apply the fee to a purchase. This is an option, but if you are going this route, rent it for several days so you have enough time to get used to it before the race. If there are folds of loose neoprene, these pockets will fill with water when you swim. This increases drag and slows you down. The wetsuit should feel snug when you put it on. It will loosen only slightly in the water.

A top-of-the-line triathlon wetsuit will fit closer to the body and allow you to swim faster than a mid-range or entry-level suit, so you get what you pay for in speed. But the wetsuit should be comfortable too. Beginners should place comfort before speed, then upgrade as their experience and skill level increases.

Wetsuit manufacturers make wetsuits in three price ranges: entry level, mid-range and top-of-the-line. A top-end wetsuit will be made of softer neoprene and have strategically placed panels, channels and rough surfaces that maximize grip on the water in some places and water flow in others. No matter which price range you choose, compare suits from several manufacturers. The speed benefits are fairly uniform in each price range, so choose the suit that feels the best.

The speed and warmth advantages are reduced if your wetsuit doesn't have sleeves. If you are doing an extremely short race (less than 400m of swimming), it may be impractical to spend the time removing a wetsuit. The longer the race is, the greater the benefit of wearing a wetsuit. A speed suit is a good option for short races or races where wetsuits are not allowed. They provide a speed benefit by reducing drag and are easier to remove than a wetsuit. However, be careful about the regulations for wear during races. Aside from water temperature issues, USAT and World Triathlon Corporation (Ironman) have prohibitions concerning various materials and a new limit on wetsuit thickness (not to exceed 5 mm), which will be phased in by 2013. The regulations are essentially in line with FINA and ITU rules.

WHEN TO WEAR YOUR WETSUIT

HOW TO PUT YOUR WETSUIT ON

Putting on a wetsuit sounds simple, but it really isn't (especially the first time). These tips should help:

1. Be patient when you put it on. It might take 10 minutes to get into.
2. Stay cool and dry. It is more difficult if you are sweaty or wet.
3. Bring someone experienced with you. It may feel awkward to ask a store clerk for advice on fit.
4. Clip your nails and treat your wetsuit as if it is as delicate as tissue paper.

It is very easy to cut through the material, so be careful and patient.

5. You can't pull it on like a pair of jeans. Put it over your ankles then pull it from the inside of the suit up over your claves and legs. The inside of the suit is more resistant to fingernails than the soft outside surface.

6. Once you have it on, you will have to spend a few more minutes fine tuning the fit. If your wetsuit doesn't fit right, you should try to exchange it for one that does. Once it is yours, there are things you can do to customize it, but altering the suit will void the warranty.

Box 8. How to make your wetsuit fit just right

First pull it over your legs to your waist. Then bend down and pull and pull it up a few inches at a time, up your calf, to the knee, to the thigh and over the hips. Go all the way around your leg front, back and sides and pull it up higher on your crotch than you think is necessary. Squat down like a Sumo wrestler and stand back up. If the wetsuit is still in the right place you are ready to move on to the top half.

Put your arms in the sleeves and pull small pinches of it up and all around your arms to your shoulders. Your arms and shoulders need the most mobility so this area should be as loose as possible before you pull the suit all the way over your shoulders.

Once it is over your shoulders, pull it up around your torso to your neck, pulling it up as high as you can for maximum mobility. If it is pulling down on the shoulder or the neck is too tight, start at the calf and shimmy the suit back all the way up from calf to knee to thigh, etc, pulling folds up as you would put on pantyhose, a little at a time. This is a common problem if you are tall or chunky. You may end up having the leg opening a bit higher on your calf rather than at the ankle but that is alright.

If you feel a lack of mobility in the shoulders, start at the wrist and work the suit back up your arm all the way to your neck. Pulling up like this will shorten your sleeves but it is more important to have plenty of shoulder mobility.

If the sleeves or legs are too long, you can cut the excess off, but altering the suit will void the warranty. If the neck opening hits you in the wrong spot, you can get creative and either roll it down securing it into position with wetsuit glue, or you can remove the excess.

LEARN IN IT

The benefits of swimming often in a wetsuit are greatest for new or nervous swimmers. Learning to swim in a full wetsuit from day one gives an athlete instant buoyancy, allowing the cultivation of relaxed, race-specific swim mechanics right away. It also helps the athlete habituate to the sensation of being cocooned in neoprene as he swims. Once you have achieved a level of competence, take the wetsuit off and adjust to swimming without it so you can train in a heated pool without getting overheated.

WEAR IT OFTEN

Train regularly with your wetsuit to get used to the sensations while wearing it and to build confidence and speed. It is important to wear your wetsuit for the entire race distance at race pace at least once before your race. You may not experience any tight spots or chaffing if you swim a few laps, but the race distance may reveal problem areas. Figure out where it rubs and where it tends to stick when you pull it off. Apply Body Glide or another lubricant to those areas. See Box 9.

Box 9. Common lubrication areas for wetsuit comfort

- Jawline – to prevent chaffing from shoulder contact as you stroke.
- Neck – front, back and sides – to prevent chaffing.
- Top of shoulder – to prevent chaffing.
- Armpit front and back – to prevent chaffing.
- Cuffs – to speed removal.
- Calves – to speed removal.
- Heels – to speed removal.

It is a colossal waste of time to hone your swimming skills to perfection and then have to change them on race day. But that is exactly what happens once you get into open water in a wetsuit. How many times do you see triathletes splashing and kicking the air *above* the water line because they haven't adjusted their kick to their new buoyancy? How many over-rotate on race day, disturbing the subtle sense of balance that is ingrained from non-wetsuited laps? These are examples of wasted energy that can be overcome by practicing in your wetsuit.

Notice the various panels, seams and surfaces on it. Take the time to figure out what each component is for and make sure you have the wetsuit adjusted right so you can exploit its speed-enhancing benefits. It takes more than a single wearing to learn the nuances of your wetsuit.

Depending on air and water temperature, wearing your wetsuit for an entire workout can put you at risk for overheating. Instead, you can and should wear it for part of your session on a regular basis. Indeed, many pools go unheated during the winter months and using your wetsuit makes those and open water venues available for training.

Pool chemicals can shorten the life of a wetsuit, but less so if you rinse it well and let it dry between wearings. Wearing your wetsuit more often will shorten its life, but it won't necessarily cost you more. The high cost of pool access and Master's Swimming can make it cheaper to replace your wetsuit once a year than to pay a fee for every workout in a heated pool.

RACE DAY

TIMING

Practicing in your wetsuit also allows you to get good at the first event of any triathlon — getting your wetsuit on. Remember to put your timing chip against your skin, not over your wetsuit. You will have a hard time removing your wetsuit with the timing chip on and it could come off without you realizing it.

Before race day, you should determine how long it takes to put on your wetsuit and get it adjusted just right. The main fitting is accomplished on land, then the fine adjustments are done in the water. You must know this so that you can time things right on race day.

Typically, the elites go in the first wave, then the younger to older men and women. If it is a hot summer day and you are swimming in one of the later waves, it is foolish to put on your wetsuit and sit around stewing in it (becoming dehydrated in the process) for 45 minutes before your wave starts.

It is also unwise to have to rush into your wetsuit and immediately start your race without adequate time to make the right adjustments and to warm up.

The more often you put your wetsuit on, the more comfortable and confident you will be with the process. Practice often so you will have one less thing to worry about.

EFFICIENCY

A wetsuit will keep you warm and relatively comfortable in cold water. The combination of buoyancy, a slick surface, reduced drag and reduced oxygen consumption at any given speed (2, 3) means you will go faster with less effort. This is especially important if you are doing Ironman-distance races or need to shave every second off your time to get to the podium. It is also true that the leaner you are, the more you will benefit from the floatation of a wetsuit.

PROTECTION

Wetsuits do more than make you fast. They also provide a psychological and physical barrier between you and the flora and fauna of the water. It insulates you from the sensation of grass or kelp sliding along your body and it makes the inevitable body contact with other swimmers less personal. Think of it as a protective barrier between you and the elements.

Your wetsuit should be comfortable and comforting. If your wetsuit feels constrictive, it either needs to be adjusted more carefully or it is the wrong size.

REMOVAL

As you are trotting to T1, reach back and open the zipper all the way. This is difficult but it gets easier with practice.

Don't stop to drain water that has collected in the suit. It will make removal much more difficult.

Pull the wetsuit down over your shoulders to your waist as you enter T1. As soon as you reach your bike, pull it down over your hips. Once it is below the hips, sit on the ground and pull it off your calves and over your heels. Many triathletes attempt to remove their wetsuits while standing but by doing so risk losing their balance and bumping into other athletes or their pricey tri bikes. If you place a folded towel in the right spot next to your bike, you can plop right down onto it and pull your wetsuit off. The towel will absorb some of the water from your shorts before you get onto the bike and you will protect your wetsuit and shorts from the rough ground.

Some races have volunteers who will help you remove your wetsuit (wetsuit strippers). Typically, they wait in a carpeted area just beyond the swim finish. It is best to have your wetsuit unzipped already when you reach them. The next step is pulling the front down over your shoulders off your arms and chest. The volunteers will help you. As soon as the suit is below your hips, lay down and the wetsuit stripper will forcefully pull the suit off over your feet. The whole process takes only a few seconds, and it is always amusing.

ARE WETSUITS DANGEROUS?

Overheating is a dangerous possibility that has caused the death of at least one triathlete during a race (see Appendix D). Swimming the race distance in the pool is fine as long as you feel comfortable. Don't train so long and hard that you begin to feel uncomfortably warm. You can get your wetsuit practice in by wearing it for a few hundred yards at a time over several workouts. Take it off when you begin to feel overly warm

Theoretically it is possible that a poorly fitting wetsuit could be dangerous for certain people in unusual circumstances, but there is no reason to fear that your wetsuit will cause you problems if it fits right. I am not aware of any research indicating that wetsuits are dangerous. That said, if you take time to achieve a good fit and practice often yet you still feel uncomfortable in your wetsuit, then don't race in it.

HABITUATION TO COLD WATER

Lynne Cox has pushed the cold water swimming envelope to extremes. She swam 1.2 miles in 32°F water without a wetsuit. But for the rest of us, water becomes unbearably cold at about 50° degrees.

Considering that water drains heat from your body 60 times faster than air, cold water becomes dangerous in a very short time. The thermal receptors on your face respond by reflex to cold water, forcing the blood vessels in the extremities to contract so that the warm blood is preserved where it is needed most, in the trunk and head. You gasp and hold your breath for a moment. The heart rate decreases and blood pressure goes up then hyperventilation follows. These reactions are known as cold water shock. After the first moments, the body habituates to a level of controlled alarm, and you can swim. The colder the water is, the more profound the response and the faster your body temperature plunges. Your thinking ability and motor skills become impaired, and even an expert swimmer will soon drown if the water is cold enough.

Cold water is nothing to mess with. Triathletes usually wear wetsuits in races, but the wetsuits are designed more for speed and buoyancy than for warmth.

Even with a wetsuit, you will experience cold water shock when you put your face into the water. These reactions can cause panic if you are already apprehensive about being in the water. Remember that it is important to minimize the sense of shock you feel when you get into open water and one of the things you can do is to get your body used to cold water well before you have to race. Box 10 has an exercise that may help you Habituate to cold water.

COLD WATER AND COLD WEATHER RACING

USAT coaches Mary DeLaney, PT, and Allen DeLaney, MD, ME, are owners of Rehab to Racing, whose mission is to rehabilitate and coach injured athletes or athletes who want to remain uninjured. They look at their clients from a medical perspective but through an athlete's eye. Mary and Allen are age group-competitive triathletes with multiple podium placings, and they have graciously provided the following tips for cold water racing.

"Put your wetsuit on early! Do not even THINK about wearing a sleeveless wetsuit! Keep your fleece cap on as well as your socks and shoes. Watch other triathletes shivering with goose bumps and even purplish extremities and other signs of early

hypothermia. Your full wetsuit is far warmer than even two sweatshirts. If you are still cool, put your warm-up jacket and pants on over your full wetsuit. Forget flip-flops, wear your shoes.

Beg, borrow or steal a neoprene wetsuit cap. These are great cold water devices. Get one that looks like a racing swim cap with a chin strap. Don't get a full hood. Put the neoprene cap on under your colored swim cap. The blood vessels to your head can't constrict with cold exposure, so your head becomes a major avenue for heat loss in cold water. You may also need to consider neoprene socks (not booties) if the water temperature is projected to be less than 60°.

Before race day, find out whether the water temperature you'll be swimming in makes you dizzy. As water temperatures fall below 65°F, many swimmers experience dizziness due to cold water entering their ears. If you get dizzy, you will need to swim with some form of earplugs. You should experiment in the pool and find out which ones work best for you.

Take a large (e.g., 1 qt.) disposable bottle of warm water to the swim start. Stow it in the middle of your gear bag to keep it warm. About 5 minutes before you enter the water, pour it down the neck of your wet suit. Make sure it is not hot enough to burn you. The warm water in your suit will prevent the rush of cold water into the suit when you start swimming.

Avoid a swimming warm-up. Most likely this will only make you colder as you wait for your wave to be called. Instead, warm up with a short run. Then, less than 5-7 minutes before your wave start, thoroughly splash water on your face or dunk your face in the water several times. Get your face and neck used to the water temperature."

WETSUIT RULES

Wetsuits have extended the triathlon season by making cold water swims tolerable. The International Triathlon Union (ITU) and USA Triathlon (USAT) have both adopted guidelines to allow wetsuit use during triathlons based on athletic status (elite or not), swim length, and water temperature (see Box 11).

Box 11. Water temperature standards for wearing wetsuits in triathlon

ITU Rules(4):
Age Group 300m-1500m (Sprint): Wetsuits mandatory in water below 14°C (57.2°F) and forbidden in water above 20°C (68°F).
Age Group: 3000m-4000m (Olympic-Iron distance): Wetsuits mandatory in water below 16°C (60.8°F) and forbidden in water above 22°C (71.6°F).
Elite 750m-1500m (Sprint): Wetsuits mandatory in water below 14°C (57.2°F) and forbidden in water temperature above 22 °C (71.6°F).
Elite 3000m (Olympic distance): Wetsuits mandatory in water below 15°C (59°F) and forbidden in water temperature above 23° C (73.4°F).
Elite 4000m (Ironman Distance): Wetsuits mandatory in water below 16°C (60.8°F) and forbidden in water temperature above 24 °C (75.2°F).

USAT Rules(5):
Age Group: Wetsuits allowed in water temperature up to 78°F (26°C).
Optional between 78°F (26°C) and below 84°F(28.9°C) but athlete not eligible for award.
Not permitted in water 84°F (28.9°C) and above.
Elite: Wetsuits allowed in water temperature up to 78°F (26°C) in races under 3000m and up to 71.6°F(22°C) in races 3000m and longer.

World Triathlon Corporation has adopted similar rules in compliance with FINA and ITU:
Wetsuits may be worn in water temperatures up to and including 24.5 degrees Celsius/76.1 degrees Fahrenheit.
Athletes who choose to wear a wetsuit in water temperatures exceeding 24.5 degrees C /76.1 degrees F will not be eligible for awards, including World Championship slots.
Wetsuits will be prohibited in water temperatures greater than 28.8 degrees C/84 degrees F

On the subject of regulations, the governing bodies in the world of triathlon have adopted additional rules relating to wetsuit materials and thickness (Box 12).

Box 12. Rules relating to Wetsuit Materials and Thickness

World Triathlon Corporation (Ironman) US Rules Regarding Swimwear (6):

- Swimwear and swim apparel must be comprised of 100 percent textile material, such as nylon or lycra, and may not include rubberized material such as polyurethane or neoprene.

- Swimwear may not cover the neck or extend past the shoulders or knees.

- Swimwear may contain a zipper.

- A race kit or trisuit may be worn underneath swimwear.

- Wetsuits cannot measure more than 5 millimeters thick. USAT has adopted this rule and will apply to races starting in 2013(7).

© Bakke-Svensson/Ironman

CHAPTER 9
Water Skills

Master these skills in the pool with and without your wetsuit. Then read Chapter 10 before returning to work through these skills in open water.

USE THE TOOLS AS YOU LEARN THE SKILLS

Section 1 provided you with tools to calm your body and mind. Don't wait until race day to try them. The best time to practice them is now, while you are learning the Fearless Swimming Skills. Master the skills first in the pool, with and without your wetsuit. Incorporate the tools when you need them to master the skills.

You probably won't be afraid in the pool, so practicing with strategies to calm you down might seem like a waste of time, but it is not. You have to practice taking control when you aren't afraid so that you are able to take control on race day when you are afraid.

Ideally, you will have already become familiar with belly breathing and have worked through the habituation exercises. As a rule, you should have at least two of the mindset and focusing strategies in mind when you begin to work through these drills.

Some of the skills will seem ridiculously easy. Do them anyway. Pay special attention to the difficult ones. Practice them until they are so easy that you get bored, then move on.

SKILL #2: MASS STARTS

There are three components to the mass start:
1. Positioning yourself correctly in relation to the natural conditions (waves, current, etc.) and within the crowd,
2. Getting into the water and establishing a swimming rhythm, and
3. Using effective techniques to deal with swimming in a mob.

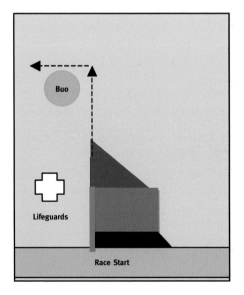

POSITIONING

Chapter 10 describes how natural conditions should influence your starting position. Being in the right spot in terms of the crowd is simpler; either lead, follow, or get out of the way!

Figure 7. Position of swimmers at start of race

Figure 7 shows a typical positioning of swimmers from the start line to the first buoy. The fastest swimmers are up at the front (red), favoring the shortest line to the buoy. Seasoned, confident athletes start in the middle (purple). Beginners usually start in the back and favor the outside (black) to avoid the mob.

Unfortunately, beginners with poor pacing and navigation skills invariably seed themselves in the beginning and middle of the pack. They start out too fast, then create obstructions for everyone behind them when they implode and start swimming in the wrong direction. It is nearly impossible to avoid running over these swimmers.

Likewise, faster swimmers often seed themselves in the back to avoid being run over. When the gun goes off, they tend to swim over others in front of them.

The only ones that don't have to deal with these problems are the very fastest swimmers.

Fearless swimmers who know how to swim straight and navigate effectively should start at the inside (green) edge. The only people there are usually lifeguards who want to keep the racers from cutting inside the buoy so you get a fairly clear path to swim in. The lifeguards also serve as helpful sighting marks.

ENTRY TECHNIQUES

BEACH STARTS

To practice a beach start, make sure you know if there are any obstructions, debris or holes in the shallows. Then put on your wetsuit, warm up, and stand around for a few minutes. Jump up and down a little to get your heart rate elevated before the imaginary gun goes off, then go. Swim hard for 50 strokes to get your heart rate up further, then settle into a race-pace rhythm.

DEEP WATER STARTS

You can easily practice deep water starts in a pool. Just start swimming without pushing off from the wall.

On race day, your wetsuit makes it easy to tread water or just float for a while before the gun goes off. The challenge is in staying warm enough if the water is cold, and keeping your heart rate up just a little so that you don't lose the benefit of your warm-up. You can move your legs a bit, but don't get them fatigued or you may risk cramping later on. You can scull with your arms, too, or change positions, frequently rolling from stomach to back.

If you have an important race with a deep water start, get used to waiting around in deep water for up to 10 minutes.

DOCK OR BOAT STARTS

Diving off a pool deck with your goggles on will simulate a dock or boat start. Here are some tips for keeping your goggles in place:

- Pull the strap so they fit snuggly.
- Flatten the strap around the back of your head and separate the straps if there are two of them.
- Wear your cap over your goggles strap.
- Wear low-profile goggles that fit under your brow line and have a rounded, rather than squared-off lens.
- Tuck your chin into your chest so the water impacts the top of your head, not your brow line.

INS AND OUTS

Ins and outs are a common drill done to simulate the race start and finish. The idea is to begin at an imaginary start line, careen into the water and swim a few yards all out to send your heart rate up, then turn around and swim hard to the beach and run to an imaginary transition area.

The main benefit of this drill is becoming familiar with the high exertion of the race start and finish. If you have some friends join you, there is the added benefit of dealing with a crowd.

MOB SWIMMING

Learning to swim in a mob starts with getting the gang into the water and swimming together in close quarters. From there, you can progress to near-race experiences in small doses as described in Chapter 2. Here's how to get started.

Find two or more friends and get into a single lane in the pool. Practice three abreast, bumping and swimming over each other. Sprint to the end. Take turns with one of you behind, two ahead. Have the person in the back swim over the two in front to take the lead. It is helpful to learn how to deal with someone swimming over you because eventually it will happen in a race. When you practice this with people you know, it is all in good fun. Try to have that same attitude when it happens on race day. If someone swims over you, it is not because they want to, it is because they are forced to by other swimmers that you probably don't see. Don't get angry. Be as fluid as you can both mentally and physically.

Expect body contact. Be grateful for the buffer of your wetsuit and stay loose and compliant. If you get banged around, try to relax and go with it and, of course, be gentle with others as you come into contact with them.

If you want to learn to appreciate triathlon swimming, try doing laps across a pool without lane lines, that is crowded with kids and recreational swimmers, without plowing into anyone. Look out for others above and below the water's surface. Breathe on both sides. Five minutes of this is a fine introduction to the dodging, stops and starts you may encounter in a triathlon. Doing this regularly will improve your ability to anticipate and take evasive action. The abrupt changes in body position are also a good challenge for your muscles. If you start to feel a cramp coming on, you know where to direct more effort in the gym.

Swimming for five minutes across a play pool like this is even harder than swimming in a triathlon. At least on race day, everyone is (hopefully) moving in the same direction.

SKILL #3: DOLPHIN DIVING

Dolphin diving or "dolphining" is a fast way to move through water that is knee to hip deep. It is most often used in the ocean as a way to quickly get through surf, but it can be used anywhere. It is fast but very tiring. It is great to know how to do it, but that doesn't mean you have to use it on race day. It is perfectly fine to wade into the water and begin swimming right away.

Dolphining is fastest in shallower water because you can use your legs to drive you forward rather than up in order to clear the water. You can practice in water up to your chest, but it has no speed advantage at that depth. If you are tall enough, you can practice in the shallow end of the pool. Follow your outstretched hands and dive down. When your hands touch bottom, pull your knees under you and plant your feet under you like a frog. Then extend your arms as you push forward and up from the bottom. The deeper the water is, the harder you have to push.

When you break the surface, keep your hands fully extended and your head tucked. Snatch a breath and dive down again. Repeat. Spend a few minutes racing around the shallows this way for a great cardiovascular and leg workout (think explosive squats).

Photo 7. Dolphining

In the open water, don't start dolphining until you know what is under you. Be careful about submerged rocks or tree stumps. If your feet get stuck in the mud or there is debris on the bottom, you are better off swimming right away.

SKILL #4: BILATERAL BREATHING

Fearless swimmers are versatile. Being able to breathe on both sides allows you to see above and below the surface of the water in both directions. Sometimes this is enough to keep you on course, and it can help you avoid bumping into other swimmers. You lift your head less, so you slow down less, too.

Breathing on both sides dramatically improves stroke, even though it can be uncomfortable at first. You may have a hard time getting a breath or keeping water out of your nose. Try the "Water in the Nose" exercise in Chapter 3 if you have trouble. Sometimes you will breathe more on one side than another because of the conditions or because it helps you swim straighter (more on that later).
When you are learning to breathe on a new side, keep your lead hand fully extended a beat longer than usual when you take a breath. To breathe on the left, keep your right arm extended. To breathe on the right, keep the left arm extended.

At first you should do entire laps on your new side. This will force you to adjust. Next, alternate one lap on your familiar side and one lap on your new side. When you are comfortable with that, alternate sides with each breath. Breathe right, stroke, stroke, breathe left, stroke, stroke, etc.

SKILL #5: DRAFTING

Swimming in a drafting position can significantly improve subsequent cycling efficiency and could therefore improve triathlon performance overall. A study in France tested the effect of swimming directly behind another swimmer and found such benefits as lower rate of perceived exertion (RPE) after the swim, 7% lower heart rate values during the final four minutes of the swim, significantly lower post-swim lactate values, significantly lower VO2, heart rate and lactate values on the bike, and even slightly improved cycling efficiency (1).

If lane lines are installed in the pool, you can simulate the close quarters by swimming two or even three abreast in a lane. Practice in different draft positions near the lead swimmer. The most effective places are either a few inches off and behind the leader's shoulder, or directly behind their feet. The closer you are to them the better, but there is still benefit up to 4 meters behind another swimmer.

Drafting behind a swimmer who is going slightly faster than you is a benefit, but only if the lead swimmer is going in the right direction and only if you are comfortable with swimming close to other swimmers. However, those are big ifs.

Choose your leader carefully or the benefit will be eaten up by the extra distance you cover. How do you find the right leader? On race day, you should look for swimmers somewhat ahead of you who seem to be going straight for the buoy. Set your sights on one and take a few harder strokes to catch up. Take your race goals into account when you select your pace. Getting into a draft position allows you to go faster with less effort, but you still have to go fast enough to stay with the leader. If the lead swimmer is going too fast, you will still use more energy than you planned. For an Ironman race, this could be a mistake, but for a sprint, you probably are not concerned about saving yourself for the rest of the race.

In some races, the congestion is such that you will always be swimming behind and alongside others. It may seem like you are getting nowhere, but you will benefit from being swept along this way as long as you are in a group that is moving well enough.

If your little pod of swimmers is moving too slowly, either back off or swim ahead to get into a faster group. Don't bat the lead swimmer in the feet repeatedly. It is a good way to get kicked in the face.

SKILL #6: SIGHTING

Sighting is looking to see where you are going. The best position in swimming is with your head down, maintaining a level vessel that glides through the water. Sighting is a necessary part of navigation so strive to do it without disturbing your body alignment.

Lifting your head up makes your feet sink. It is strenuous, and it can give you a stiff neck. The more you do it, the slower and more prone to motion sickness you may become. A fearless swimmer navigates with what he sees above the water *and* below, as well as in front, to the side and behind him.

Race day buoys are among the most difficult objects to sight because they are always hard to see from the water. Large landmarks are easier to see and they are a good alternative, but don't stop there. Use lifeguards, paddleboards, boats, the shoreline, other single swimmers (especially the ones who lift their heads incessantly) and clusters of swimmers to keep yourself on course.

No matter how good you are at looking to the side, you will have to look forward, too. There are three ways to do it:

1. Swim with your head up high, like a water polo player, for a few strokes. You should be able to breathe while looking forward. This affords a good view but should be used sparingly because it is strenuous and the higher you lift your head, the more your feet will sink. This is necessary on very choppy days when you can't see over the swells.

2. Lift your head just enough that your eyes clear the surface as in Photo 7. Take as many strokes as necessary to find your way. Then, when you need to breathe, roll to your side to take a breath and continue with your normal swimming stroke.

3. Breathe to the side first, then turn your face forward for a glance before putting it back into the water.

Practice to improve your comfort and efficiency in these positions.

If you are swimming in the ocean, it is helpful to be able to sight behind you so you can see the waves coming up behind you. See more about this in Chapter 11.

Each of these methods takes some practice and muscle conditioning. Incorporate some sighting into your regular workouts so you can do it smoothly and don't end up with a stiff neck on race day.

Photos 8 & 9. Two views of Total Immersion's Terry Laughlin lifting his head just enough to see, with nose and mouth remaining underwater as he maintains a straight body line.
Used with the permission of Total Immersion Swimming.

SKILL #7: SWIMMING STRAIGHT

It is also important to learn to swim as straight as possible. You can practice in the pool by swimming with your eyes closed, but it is unnerving to swim knowing that you will soon bump into a lane line. Another way to accomplish the same thing is to swim against a tether with your eyes closed. This way you don't actually cover any distance, and you won't bump into anything until you have gone more than 90 degrees off course. It becomes clear in very short order if you are pulling to one side.

Box 13 has instructions for using a tether to teach yourself to swim straight.

You can purchase various tethers online or make one yourself. Attach a resistance tube or a bungee cord to an old belt, then anchor it to a handrail at the pool. It helps if the tether has clips on both ends because if you tie a knot, you can pull it really tightly as you swim making it hard to untie. If you use a knot, tie a double figure-eight loop so you can untie it.

Box 13. Using a tether

Start swimming and position yourself over or just behind a marker on the bottom of the pool (or put a weight or a rock on the bottom).

Close your eyes and count 10 strokes then open them again. Have you moved to one side or the other? Try it a few times. If you consistently stay at the same place for 10 strokes you can be confident that on race day you can wait at least 10 strokes between head-lifts for sighting.

Try it with 20 strokes, then 30. How many strokes does it take for you to start to veer off?

Do you tend to turn in the same direction each time?

If, for example, you tend to move to the left after 10 stokes, practice correcting that with your eyes closed as you swim against the tether. Count your strokes and every 8th one pull harder on the left. Does this keep you straight?

Experiment until you can consistently swim 20 stokes in a straight line with your eyes closed, then try for 30.

SKILL #8: TURNS

Lakes, rivers and oceans don't come equipped with a wall to push-off from. In a race, you have to use your body to turn so it is best to get used to doing this in a pool first.

Sharp, deep water turns require you to alter body position in ways that encourage calf and hamstring cramping. Regular practice will improve your technique and alert you to gaps in your muscle conditioning. If you feel a cramp coming on, spend extra time on that muscle in the gym.

Swim 200 yards (eight laps) but turn around before you get to the wall and don't push off. You will probably never make eight turns in a triathlon swim, but it is good practice. If lane lines have been removed, you can swim diagonally across, which means you can no longer follow the black line. This gives you practice swimming in a straight line as well.

You can also swim around the edges of a pool with lane lines removed. As you approach a corner, turn 90 degrees. Open water swimmers call this "pool open water" and set up buoys in the corners of the pool, racing around the periphery. This is a great way to swim continuously without a wall to push off or lane lines to smooth out the water. Give it a try when you get a chance.

SKILL #9: 3-SPEEDS

Chances are that you have one swim speed that feels the best. It is helpful to develop several; an easy warm-up pace (slow), a moderate steady pace you can maintain for awhile (moderate) and a faster pace to get you out of tough spots, like the crowd around the buoy (fast). You probably practiced going slow and moderate speeds already, but you should learn to go fast too, even if you don't plan to do it on race day.

Fearless swimmers in training sometimes can't resist dashing into the water and going all out for the first 100 yards, despite their good intentions. The extra splashing can throw your breathing off and, combined with the adrenaline rush, your heart rate will soar. This is when your wetsuit starts to feel extra tight and you may start to feel panicky.

You must practice swimming hard in your wetsuit before race day so that you are familiar with all of these sensations.

SKILL #10: FINISH TO T1

Going from swimming to running can be very disorienting and strenuous. The more time you spend swimming, the harder it is to get vertical again. It is common to feel dizzy and short of breath even if you weren't swimming exceptionally hard. The dizziness can be worse in cold water so try earplugs if this is a problem for you.

The finish of your race begins with rounding the final buoy and figuring out where the finish line is. This is where some pre-race planning pays off. Find a large landmark or two near the finish line so you can find it quickly.

The ins and outs drill described earlier will help you with some aspects of finishing but you should also practice a race finish every time you swim in open water.

You can practice the outs in your pool, going from swimming to jogging up the pool steps. Ideally, you will be able run a few hundred yards to a mock transition area, unzipping your wetsuit as you go but this may not be possible in your pool set-up, especially when running is discouraged. Do the best you can while staying within the safety parameters.

On race day, you should stand up until you hit the bottom with your hands. Pull your goggles up and as you run, reach around and unzip your wetsuit. Doing all of these things at once is a challenge and you will soon realize that by the time you get to T1, your heart rate will be through the roof if you don't pace yourself. You may also realize that it would be a good idea to walk barefoot more to toughen up your tender feet.

Some races finish on a beach. Others have you climb stairs or go up a ramp. Try as many of these exits as are available to you.

SKILL #11: TROUBLESHOOTING

It is important to practice what you will do if something goes wrong. You might have to stop in the middle of your race to deal with lost goggles, nausea, a cramp, anxiety or difficulty breathing. Section 1 provided some tools to help you prevent and manage these and other issues. Now is the time to practice them. Your tools are limited in the water.

What will your mental strategy be for dealing with an unexpected problem? Allow yourself to have a successful race even if you hit a rough spot.

At what point will you call for help? Read over the symptoms of cardiac and respiratory distress. Difficulty breathing that is not resolved quickly with belly breathing can indicate something more than anxiety. You should get out of the water.

- What body positions might make you more comfortable?
- Will removing your goggles and focusing on a landmark help?
- Go back over the tools for dealing with your Fear Factors and find some things you can do to help yourself in the water.

CHAPTER 10
Wild Water

USE THE TOOLS TO CALM YOUR BODY

WHERE TO START

From a mechanical standpoint, swimming in open water is not much different from swimming in the pool, but psychologically, it is a world apart. The first few strokes will convince you of that. Having mastered the fearless swimming skills in the pool should help you be more confident. You will then be well equipped for this next step.

The best way to get used to the open water is to start with the smallest venue you can find. The fearless swimming skills are best learned where you feel safe.

It might be a pond, lagoon, bay or harbor, but it is less intimidating to be in an area that feels small. If the ocean is your only option, pick a beach without surf, like one in a protected harbor. If you have a choice of lakes, choose the smallest one. When you are comfortable in a small venue, try a larger one.

Go through the fearless swimming skills with your wetsuit on, in various weather conditions. Spend extra time on the ones that are difficult and do them until you are bored. Once you master these skills in flat water, you will be ready for the next step — the surf.

HABITUATE TO MURKY WATER

Water can be eerie because it is vast, deep, and visibility can be poor, so your imagination gets the best of you. You can bump into things and things can bump into you. But triathletes can be spooked by clear water, too. Seeing objects like pier pilings and buoy lines that go down into the depths can be frightening to some.

© pierre-yves Riou, fotolia

Turn down the volume of your anxiety a notch by reducing your alarm response to impaired vision.

Your face, especially around the eyes, has special receptors that are exceptionally sensitive to cold. Merely putting your face in water arouses the sympathetic nervous system and puts you into an alarm state. Now add impaired vision to that and you increase the alarm even more. The fear makes you hyper-focused on what you can't see and on how threatened you feel. Your imagination can run away from you and once that happens, even the most innocuous object casts menace when it is distorted by sediment, algae, and microscopic creatures that make water murky.

The exercises below (Box 14) will help you to get used to swimming with impaired vision. They should be done in the pool and in open water. Stay with one step until you are entirely comfortable with it before moving on. If you wear contact lenses, you will have to modify the exercises so you can keep your goggles on, but you can still open and close your eyes as instructed. You can rub some lotion on the goggle lenses or put opaque tape on them to simulate the blurred visibility you get when you open your eyes under water without goggles.

SKILL #12: BE AWARE

When you go to the pool to swim, the environment is controlled in every way. The water temperature is regulated and it is clean, the water doesn't move, and there is nothing living in it. There is a line for you to follow, solid walls to hang onto, and lane lines ensure that you have the right amount of personal space. It is like a large bathtub.

Open water is different, challenging and fun because it is *alive*. It moves in natural directions and changes from moment to moment so you can't assume that everything is safe and under control. You should be able to evaluate possible hazards and conditions that will affect your swim. Fearless swimmers can manage in a variety of open water venues because like all skilled watermen, they are keen observers.

Box 14. Spooky water exercises

Step one: Swim in the Dark
The first thing to practice is swimming with your eyes closed in the pool, without goggles. Remember you have special receptors around your eyes and part of this task is to get those receptors stimulated so keep you goggles off for this exercise. Close your eyes under water and open them when you come up to take a breath. You can see well enough when you breathe so you won't bump into anything. Do a lap or two like this in each workout. Try it in your wetsuit too. This will help you will develop a sense of where your body is without relying on the black line. You will notice that it gets easier as you practice.

Step Two: Swim Blurry
The next step is to open your eyes underwater without goggles. If you have trouble with this, you can start with sticking your face into a large bowl of water instead of the pool . As soon as you open your eyes you will feel anxious. Don't add to it by holding your breath too long. Let some air out of your nose. Try to relax. Repeat this until you can do it without the alarm response.
 Once you have mastered this, try it in the pool for one or two laps of each workout (wetsuit too). If the pool is heavy with chemicals, have a bottle of fresh water handy at poolside so you can rinse your eyes.

Below is a list of things you should look for at various swimming venues.
In any wild water:

- Be aware of wildlife that may live in or around the water.
- Is there a designated swimming area? Buoys, ropes or flags? Warning signs? Postings about wildlife recently spotted in the area?
- Are there motorboats or other watercraft that you should avoid?
- Looking at the landscape and vegetation on the shoreline will tell you something about what to expect to find in the water. If there are large trees, there might be branches, leaves or stumps in the water. If it is dry and there are rocks and boulders on the shore, there are probably rocks in the water as well.
- Are there old fishing lines stuck in the shrubs near the water? There might be stray hooks on the bottom or tangled around vegetation in the water. Tread lightly and keep your cool if you encounter old fishing lines.
- Is there a drainage pipe, outcropping of rock, sandbars, or clumps of vegetation to avoid?

Step Three: Swim Murky

Now that you have mastered swimming in the dark and "swimming blurry", you can tackle the open water. Be sure to splash the water on your face before getting all the way in. Take the time to adjust to the cold water before you start practicing the exercises.

Sit or float in a safe, comfortable place. Put your hands on the bottom or hold onto something if you like. Start with the "swim in the dark" exercise. Since you are not swimming, you will just put your face in the water with eyes closed then turn to the side to breathe and open your eyes in the air. Get comfortable with this before the next step.

Now try to "swim blurry". Open your eyes underwater (no goggles) then turn your head to breathe. Do this until it is easy.

Next, go through the sequence again as you swim.

When you are bored with that, put on your goggles and enjoy the comfort and security of having your eyes protected ......yeah, it is still murky, but at least you can see.

- Is there debris on the shore? Be careful about broken glass and other debris.
- Deeper lakes are colder at the bottom than shallower ones. The temperature at swimming level tends to be uniform, but don't be surprised if you feel some cold spots caused by eddies churning deeper water to the surface.
- If you are going to swim in a river, it is important to look at how and in what direction the water is moving. Avoid fast moving water for training swims.
- Wild water rises and falls with rainfall, which also affects water quality and the speed of water moving downstream.
- Moving water can trap you against branches, submerged trees, dams and strainers so don't try to swim in waterways that have a noticeable current. Always keep your feet between your body and any obstructions when you are in moving water.

DIRTY WATER

Most triathletes will not experience any major illnesses from swimming in polluted waters, but it is best to avoid training in water that is contaminated. Many recreational swimming areas are tested regularly for contamination, especially in the summer months. Check with your local or regional water quality or health agencies to see if there are any warnings about particular swim venues.

Testing isn't foolproof. Water testing takes 24 to 48 hours to produce results, and many beaches re-test rather than close or issue an advisory if the results are questionable. The tests also are not designed to protect the public against all waterborne illnesses and they don't address sensitive populations like children and the elderly or those with compromised immune systems. By current EPA standards, 19 out of 1,000 people swimming in "safe" ocean water will still become ill. In the Great Lakes, the incidence is eight out of 1,000.

Exposure to bacteria, viruses, and parasites in contaminated water can cause a wide range of diseases, including ear, nose and eye infections, gastroenteritis, hepatitis, encephalitis, skin rashes, and respiratory illnesses. Experts estimate that as many as 7 million Americans get sick every year from drinking or swimming in water contaminated with bacteria, viruses or parasites. Viral gastroenteritis is the most common illness associated with swimming in polluted water. The symptoms can include chills, nausea, diarrhea, stomachache, headache and fever. Other minor illnesses can affect the eyes, ears, skin, and the upper respiratory tract.

Sources of pollution can include the following:
- Polluted storm water runoff from highways, buildings, streets and parking lots
- Sewer lines, facilities and plants
- Waste from pets, livestock and wildlife
- Poorly maintained septic tank systems
- Oil spills
- Boats or marinas that release sewage into the water

Swimming Guidelines:
1. Be aware of advisories and closures and avoid swimming in those areas.
2. Do not swim near storm drains or visible runoff.
3. Avoid swimming in water that is highly populated by seagulls, ducks or geese.
4. Clear water is better than murky water.
5. Stay out of water that smells foul.
6. Moving water is better than still water.
7. A sandy beach is better than a muddy one.
8. Avoid swimming within 72 hours after measurable rainfall.

If you must swim in water of questionable sanitation, do your best to keep the water outside of your body and to wash off as much as possible. Here are some extra precautions to take:
- Avoid ingesting water.
- Avoid swimming if you have an open wound or infection.
- Wear your wetsuit and pre-fill it with fresh, bottled water before venturing into the waterway. This will keep some of the beach/ lake water out.
- Cover open wounds with antibiotic ointment to create a barrier between the wound and the water.
- Wear a cap, goggles, nose clip and earplugs.
- When you get out of the water rinse off in fresh water (with soap if you can) and dry off, especially your ears.
- Rinse with an antibacterial mouthwash and remove your swimsuit quickly if possible.

SKILL #13: CURRENT AND CHOP

Wild water moves, and knowing how to use the movement is an advantage.
Chop is what happens to the surface of the water as wind blows across it. When there is no wind, the water is smooth and glassy. When it is stormy, the wind

creates surface waves that can crest and make foamy whitewater. Wind chop is different than surf. It can happen in lakes, ponds and of course in the ocean, too. Currents and chop will move you around, usually away from where you want to be. Figure out which direction the current is flowing and how strong it is before you start your race. Study the water. Follow the path of floating objects to see where the current takes them. Use this to anticipate how far the current will push you off course if you start directly in front of the buoy. If there is a current going across the swim course and you start your swim directly in front of the buoy, the current will push you away from it. To the extent possible, start in a location that will allow the current will push you sideways *toward the buoy* not away from it (see Figure 8).

Strong currents disturb the surface of the water. Strong currents make rapids, mild ones make ripples. It is unlikely that you will have to race up a river with a strong current but if you do, you know that going upstream will be much harder than going downstream. Plan your energy expenditure accordingly.

Some tips for swimming in current and chop:
1. Sight on tall, large landmarks. If the weather is bad, look for bright colors, too.
2. Be flexible and go with the flow. This is where bilateral breathing is invaluable. Breathe opportunistically, when you can get a clean breath, on the most advantageous side.
3. Lift your head slightly higher when sighting.
4. Swim strongly in short bursts as you go over the swells and relax when you go down between them.
5. Try to roll with the rhythm of the water rather than fighting constantly against it. Fearless swimmers enjoy the fun of it.

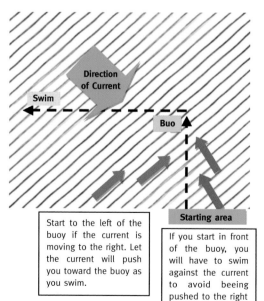

Figure 8. Effect of current on starting location.
Start to the left of the buoy if the current is moving to the right. Let the current will push you toward the buoy as you swim.

If you start in front of the buoy, you will have to swim against the current to avoid being be pushed to the right.

Start to the left of the buoy if the current is moving to the right. Let the current will push you toward the buoy as you swim.

Starting area
If you start in front of the buoy, you will have to swim against the current to avoid beeing pushed to the right

SKILL #14: NAVIGATION

The article below was provided with permission by the writer, Emmett Hines, author of Fitness Swimming (Human Kinetics), and Director and Head Coach of H2Ouston Swims. He has coached for Total Immersion, holds an ASCA Level 5 Certification, was United States Masters Swimming's Coach of the Year in 1993 and received the MACA Lifetime Achievement Award in 2002.

SWIMMING THE STRAIGHT AND NARROW (WHAT THE AVERAGE JOE DOESN'T KNOW)

by Coach Emmett Hines

Stroke ... stroke ... stroke ... stroke ... lift head ... there's the buoy ... stroke ... stroke ... stroke ... stroke ... lift head ... where's the buoy? ... stroke ... stroke ... lift head higher ... look all around ... where's that *%^&$#@ing buoy!? ... stroke ... stroke ...

You've been there, done that, still have a half-eaten Powerbar near the bottom of your equipment bag to prove it. And you are not alone. A moment of observation at any open water swim reveals that many swimmers spend a lot of time and effort "navigating."

Navigating is the polite term for the rather awkward ploy of raising one's head in mid-swim, finding a buoy, seeing how far off course one is, making a correction, putting one's face back in the water, continuing on for a few strokes and then repeating the whole affair, apparently ad infinitum. And you know, or should know, that every time you raise your head you instantly lose longitudinal balance (i.e. your hips and legs head for the bottom) thus dramatically increasing drag. And once down there, it likely takes a couple stroke cycles for them to come back up...and then its nearly time to look for the stupid buoy again.

An admittedly unscientific poll of our clients in my most recent few Total Immersion workshops leads me to believe a surprising percentage of swimmers play the buoy search game every 6 to 10 strokes of an open water swim. This means spending a majority of their swimming time very unbalanced. And numerous course corrections mean swimming farther than the entry form says. These swimmers are spending a lot of unnecessary energy on the swim.
There is a better way.

Pay attention a while longer and I'll lay out a simple strategy that will allow you to confidently swim, perhaps, 10 times as many strokes between buoy searches as you do now. But bear with me a moment as I digress...

Take your average Joe out of the pool and put him, blindfolded, in the middle of the desert and instruct him to walk in a straight line. Given no navigational information, Joe will walk in roughly a 10 mile circle. Why? Strides he takes with his right leg are just a tad shorter or longer than strides he takes with his left leg – perhaps because one leg is slightly longer than the other, perhaps different muscle strength or joint range of motion etc.

Now put Joe in open water (still blindfolded) and tell him to swim in a straight line. Guess what? He'll swim in a circle – a much smaller circle than he walks in. Like with walking in a circle, this is due to differences on the two stroking sides. Some swimmers swim in a 1-mile circle, some in a 500-yard circle, some in a 100-yard circle. Some could swim circles inside a Hyundai. The bigger the circle a swimmer naturally swims in, the less navigating he must do. If he swims in a perfectly straight line he would, theoretically, not need to navigate at all were it not for wind, currents, chop, other swimmers etc. Small-circle swimmers need to navigate a lot, regardless of conditions.

Or do they?

Joe, like every swimmer, travels a bit further, or straighter (or both) with one armstroke than with the other. Maybe he has a bit of the dreaded dropped elbow on one side and not on the other. Maybe he reaches a bit further forward on one side than on the other. Maybe he has better body roll on one side than the other. Hey, there are at least 150 things that could make the difference. But the place where the two sides seem to reach maximum divergence is when Joe breathes.

For most people, breathing is where they do something radically different than on the other strokes. Typically they lift their head to some degree. And they use the arm that should be extended weightlessly out front to, instead, push down on the water to help support the lifted head. This makes the stroke on that side much less propulsive. Swimmers often curve their back in craning the neck to breathe. Perhaps they roll more on the breathing side than on the non-breathing side. There's a long list — I won't bore you with all of it. For the average swimmer, breathing is where the biggest stroke differences are and hence where the biggest course errors are made.

Since most people breathe on just one side (every other stroke) they keep making course errors in the same direction. This makes the swimming circle small and the navigational problem big. One possible strategy would be to just alternate breathe (every third stroke) instead of one-side breathing (you *can* alternate breathe, can't you?). This could go a long way to correcting the problem. Of course this only deals with the breathing related stroke differences and wholly ignores the other stroke differences. And, alternate breathing gives you less oxygen, artificially forcing you to do the entire swim at a higher CO_2 concentration (and higher heart rate) than is necessary. You need to breathe more often than every third stroke. While alternate breathing would be a step in the right direction it still has its problems. Let's refine the strategy a bit.

Try the following in your favorite open water hole. Choose a distant object to sight on. Then close your eyes and swim 50 strokes, breathing every other stroke, then stop. See how far off course you are. Repeat several times. You should be off course by roughly the same amount each time.

Now do the same thing, breathing on your other side. You will likely be off course in the opposite direction (if not, my strategy won't work for you and you can go home) but not necessarily to the same extent. Repeat several times to see the pattern.

Then try it breathing every third stroke. After 50 strokes you'll be somewhere between the two extremes – but probably not in a straight line. Repeat several times.

Now try it again, breathing with a pattern of twice on the right side and once on the left, or vice versa (we'll call this modified alternate breathing). Then try breathing patterns of 3-and-1 or 3-and-2 or 4-and-5 etc., checking after each 50 strokes to see how far that particular breathing pattern takes you away from the straight and narrow. The idea is to gradually home in on a pattern which allows you to go 50 strokes and end up right on line. Once you've established this pattern, try going 100 strokes with the same pattern.

You now have a strategy that will allow you to forego most of the navigational interruptions to fluid swimming. Realize that the conditions in any given competition may dictate a slightly different breathing pattern than you established in the quiet solitude of your test site. However, having strategy in mind, you'll quickly be able to find a pattern that matches the prevailing conditions and thereby outsmart your competition.

© Peter Golibrzuch, fotolia

CHAPTER 11
Learn to Play in the Surf

"A white line of bubbling water surrounded us like skirts of lace, I felt as if we were swimming through New Year's Eve champagne. The bubbles tickled, and the chill made me draw in a breath and I laughed. This was a great adventure, nothing like swimming back and forth in a heated pool, following a black line and going nowhere. This was so much fun."

– Lynne Cox, Swimming to Antarctica

Surfers care a lot about waves because they are out for a good ride. Triathletes want to get past them. Fearless swimmers want to do both.

Ocean triathlons are not always in the surf. Many are held in bays, harbors and lagoons that are flat like lakes. Likewise, some lakes are so large, they actually have waves big enough to ride. If you are terrified of the surf, you can have a long and satisfying triathlon career without ever doing a race in the waves. But if you are ready to take the ultimate challenge, read on.

No two beaches are the same and surf conditions are ever changing. To master the ocean triathlon, you have to be able to evaluate surf conditions and move safely among waves. You can get lucky and bumble your way through an ocean race on a calm day, but to excel in the surf, you have to develop surf skills in their own right.

Timing is crucial. When you are learning about the surf you have the luxury of timing things to your best advantage. On race day, it is different. You may feel that you are at the mercy of the starting gun and that you will have to get in the water even if a gigantic wave is coming at you — a terrifying proposition. You may not be worried so much about going fast as you are of surviving. Granted, finding your way through the surf is not easy. But don't worry; you can still control your timing on race day. When it comes to dealing with the surf, the safest way through is usually also the fastest, too. You can have it all once you know what to do.

It is best to practice at the race venue before race day. If that is not possible, learn as much about the venue as you can and spend time in the surf whenever and wherever you can. Unlike airline tickets, ocean skills are fully transferable.

CAN YOU USE THE CALMING STRATEGIES?

The fearless swimming tools probably won't help you much as you are learning to go through the surf. The reason I say "probably" is that surflines vary. Sometimes the waves come in so slowly and gently that you have plenty of time to reflect. But often, it is a high-intensity zone even when the waves are small. You have to act quickly to avoid getting walloped.

Once you are past the surf line you will have plenty of time to implement the fearless swimming tools because at that point it is like swimming in a lake.

If you are nervous about getting into the surf at all, the safest thing you can do is to hire a personal coach or an ocean-confident friend who can literally hold your hand and guide you.

The best way to learn about the waves is to look at the process as fun, and consider the surf as a playground. Take your time and enjoy it. You will learn along the way.

BE SAFE

THE RIGHT EQUIPMENT: SURF FINS

You will never race a triathlon wearing fins. That would be cheating. But for learning about the surf in relative safety, the most effective tool is a good pair of surf fins. These fins are not for swimming long distances and they are not like the ones you may practice with in the pool. They are specially designed to give you speed and power in the waves. When you wear them, you will be able to swim much faster and this will help you get out of tight spots. Surf fins are made especially for body surfing and body boarding. The blade is stiff, there is a pocket for your foot and a strap goes over the heel. Some well-known brands include Voit Duck Feet, Viper, Da Fin (all pictured below), Churchill and POD.

Photo 10. Voit Duck Feet, Viper and Da Fin Surf Fins
Photos provided by manufacturers and used with permission

Don't wear SCUBA or skin diving fins in the surf. They won't provide the thrust or maneuverability you need, and you will probably lose them in the churning water. Investing a few dollars in a good pair of surf fins is one of the best things you can do for yourself. You will find yourself relaxing and playing in the waves in no time.

When you have mastered the surf with your fins on, you should take them off and try to do the same without them. You will instantly notice the difference in power and maneuverability, but the lessons you have learned will still apply. Eventually you should practice being in the ocean in your triathlon wetsuit, cap and goggles. You will note that the buoyancy of the wetsuit makes it tougher to slip under the waves. There may be times in the future when you forego the wetsuit on race day so you can get through the waves more easily.

CHECK SURF REPORTS

So you have a nifty pair of fins. What next? Before you head down to the beach to practice, make sure the surf conditions are mild. You can find local surf conditions online. Surf reports usually include the daily tides, water temperature, water visibility, wave size and direction, as well as warnings for incoming swells and health advisories.

These reports are especially helpful during the off-season when lifeguards are not on duty. The reports will help you decide if it is a good learning day or not before you ever get down there. If the surf is high, you will be better off waiting for a calmer day.

BEACH FLAGS

There used to be so many different flag systems at various beaches that it was confusing to the public. In 2004, the United States Lifesaving Association adopted the Standards of the International Life Saving Federation for Beach Safety and Information Flags so that the flags would be uniform. Figures 9 and 10 show the meaning of the various colors and configurations. They probably won't be flying during your early morning race, but they are very helpful on your practice days.

Figure 10. Beach Warning Flags

These flags will tell you at a glance whether it is a good day to learn in the surf or not. As a beginner, you should only go out on green flag days. If it is green flag at one beach, it is usually also green flag at all of the beaches in the vicinity.

AVOID HAZARDS

If the water seems disturbed or boils, there is probably a reef or some heavy kelp underneath. As the tide gets lower, reefs and sandbars may become exposed, and you should to adjust your movements to avoid them.

It is best to avoid rocks, reefs, jetties, docks and piers because the motion of the surf can smash you against them and the sharp sea life growing on them. The rule of thumb is to keep a cushion of water between you and any stationary object in the ocean. Lead with your feet and not your hands if you get near.

SKILL #15: TIMING

If the waves are really small, it doesn't matter so much when you try to get past them. However, if they are large enough to get your attention, timing is critical. If you can avoid the largest waves, you will get out past the surfline faster and more safely.

The best time to go out through the surf to avoid the larger waves is during the period of relative calm, known as the "lull." The lull happens right after the last wave of a "set." No matter how large the waves are on any given day, some of them will be larger and some will be smaller. The larger ones tend to arrive in groups, known as "sets." Whether it is race day or a practice day, it is important to know:

- How big the largest waves generally are. This will show you what you are in for.
- How often the sets tend to come in. Is it every 5 minutes, every 20 minutes or something in between? This will tell you how much time you have to get through the surfline before the waves get larger again.
- How many waves tend to be in each set? This will tell you how many waves in succession you will have to deal with in a worst-case scenario.

- These are important questions, but they are not rocket science. If you sit and watch the waves for a little while, you will see the patterns. Once you are familiar with the rhythm of the sets, focus your attention on where the waves are breaking. This area is known as the impact zone.

Photo 11. Triathletes Face a
Challenging Surfline
From Triathletestuff.com 2006

The size of the impact zone varies from beach to beach and watching it for a while is important because the way the waves break and the size of the impact zone determines how you will time your dash through the surfline and how difficult your journey will be.

- In a short impact zone, the waves break within 25 meters of the sand. Sometimes they break right on it. All of the action is close to shore, so if you time it right, you can get past the breakers with minimal fuss. The waves break forcefully but only in a small area. Be aggressive, and you can get through the waves quickly.

- A medium-length impact zone is anywhere from 25-50 meters. Tangling with a few waves is unavoidable but with proper timing, you may be able to avoid the larger waves.

- A long impact zone is anything longer than 50 meters, and it will take awhile to get through even if you time it right. Chances are that you will face some of the larger waves because it takes so long to get through the impact zone. The saving grace is that the waves are often mild in long impact zones. Getting through requires confidence, persistence and endurance.

SKILL #16: DIVING UNDER WAVES

Fearless swimmers see the waves as playthings. Enjoy them when you practice, but you will have to move swiftly past them when you race. Whether you are frolicking or racing, you will have to decide whether to go over, under or through every wave you encounter.

You have to know how to dive under waves. You don't have to dive under every wave, only the ones that will push you over if you try to stand against them. A wave that is nowhere near breaking is just a swell, and there is no reason to go under those. Waves that come to your knees won't give you trouble either.

Waves are circles of current like your bicycle's wheels. The current goes around and around until it bumps into the bottom. The interruption in momentum makes the wave break, just as you would fly off the front of your bike if your front wheel suddenly jammed. Don't worry though; dealing with waves is much more fun than falling off your bike.

The surface of the water is only part of the action. A wave that is 10 feet high will bump into the bottom in water that is 10 feet deep. Thus, larger waves break in deeper water. On some beaches, the water depth increases gradually. You can tell because you will see small waves breaking far away from the beach (long impact zone). At other beaches, it gets deep very quickly and you will see good-sized waves breaking almost on dry sand (short impact zone).

Diving under a wave allows you to pass under the current and avoid its wrath. It is scary at first, so start with small surf and be sure to keep your arms stretched in front of you. If you don't dive deep enough, you will get caught up in the current and get sloshed around. If the waves are large enough, you will get pummeled. Anyone who has been pounded by a big one knows it is no fun. Be sure to start your dive early so that you can get completely under the wave before it hits you. Timing is tricky because as the wave approaches, the surge pulls you toward it. Things happen quickly. Start your dive sooner than you think necessary. If the waves are large, dive even sooner. Give yourself time to get well under the wave bearing down on you.

How deep should you dive? Dive as deep as possible. Remember, you must get under the wheel and what you see on the surface is only half of it. You need to dive at least as deep as the wave is tall. Once you get under the wave, stay there a little longer than you think necessary. Use your momentum and move forward underwater as the wave passes over. If you feel the bottom, use it to pull yourself forward. If you come up too soon you may get caught in the current and dragged backwards. Practice a lot and soon you will be an expert.

SKILL #17: USING RIPTIDES

As waves break, water is pushed on shore, reaching up the beach before it recedes. When a set of large waves comes in, more water is pushed up the beach. When the waves come in rapid succession, the water doesn't have a chance to go out before more is pushed on shore. Eventually, gravity takes over and the surplus finds its way back out to sea at a low point in the landscape. The water moves fast like a river, churning up the sand. This is current is known as a riptide, runout, rip current or rip (Figure 11).

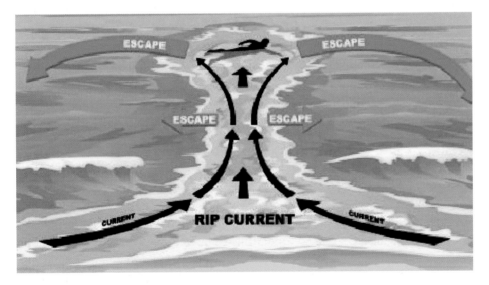

Figure 11. Illustration of a rip current adapted from signs posted on United States beaches

Riptides happen constantly, even when the waves are small. A small riptide might be 2-4 meters wide and extend out to sea only 10 meters or so. This is so small you might not even notice it.

When the surf is large, the riptides are larger and stronger. A huge riptide can be 25 meters wide and extend 50 meters into the ocean. Swimming directly against a riptide is like swimming upstream; it is tiring and not very productive. Don't do it unless you want the lifeguard to rescue you.

If you want to get out of the riptide, swim parallel to the shore across the riptide until you are in less tumultuous water, then go back to the beach. The other option is to relax and let the riptide carry you out to the end, then return to the beach away from the rip through clear water.

There is nothing inherently dangerous about a riptide unless you don't know how to swim in the ocean. A person who is unaware that they are moving out to sea may suddenly face waves they are not expecting, which may cause them to panic and have a hard time getting back to shore.

A riptide is sometimes called an "undertow" but that is a misnomer. Riptides move out to sea, not down to the bottom. Undertow is another name for a surge that pulls you toward an approaching wave right before it breaks. If you happen to be a small child, it can pull you off your feet and drag you into the oncoming wave, which can be deadly.

If you are fortunate enough to spot a riptide that is traveling from the vicinity of the start line out in the direction of the buoy on race day, it may be worthwhile to swim in the riptide instead of trying to avoid it. If you think you are ready to ride a rip, practice first at a guarded beach in smaller surf. Once mastered, use this technique on race day to take minutes off your swim.

SKILL #18: BODYSURFING

Bodysurfing is an art so don't expect this book will make you into a beautiful bodysurfer. The best to hope for is an elementary level of competence. If you can ride a wave or two into the shore, you can have an exhilarating ride, which will save you some effort and whisk you past the other competitors. It is free speed.

Riding waves is complex because so much goes into choosing the right wave and being in the right place at the right time. Once you have that, you still have to do all the correct things with your body. Developing the subtle skills of bodysurfing takes time.

With realistic expectations, here are the basics:

Waves are often defined by where they break (shorebreak, reefbreak, etc.) but that doesn't tell a beginner the most important thing; Is the wave one that a beginner can ride?

If the wave is breaking on dry sand, the answer is "no." If the wave is breaking over rocks, the answer is also "no." If the wave is so big it scares you, the answer is again, "no."

You should learn on small waves that break in a few feet of water on a sandy beach. Look around, if it is the swimming season and no one is bodysurfing at your location, that could mean the waves aren't right for it. You might have to try a different place.

The next issue is whether the shape of the wave lends itself to riding. The shape of the wave is determined mostly by the seascape beneath it. That is why at some beaches the waves are considered "good" and at other beaches they aren't. What makes a particular wave good for riding depends upon your vehicle. A good wave for a longboard can be different than a good wave for a shortboard, and waves that are great fun for bodsysurfers can be impossible for surfers to ride.

Bodysurfing allows you to use the wave's momentum to get to the beach. Skilled bodysurfers ride sideways across the face of the wave like surfers and bodyboarders do. This kind of bodysurfing is great, but it isn't particularly helpful on race day. Your goal is to get to the beach as soon as possible, and when you ride across waves (instead of down the front of them) you have to tuck out and under the back of the wave to avoid a wipeout at the end. Those skills won't get you to the finish line any sooner.

The most functional style of bodysurfing for a triathlete is riding a wave straight in with your body in a prone position (lying on your stomach). Keep your head low, facing forward but above water for the whole ride. Ride as far up the beach as is practical, but not so far that you are left sprawled on dry sand like a beached whale. When the water is shallow enough, stand up and run to T1.

START WITH WHITEWATER

The easiest way to get the feel of riding waves is to ride the ones that have already broken and are tumbling to shore as whitewater. Start with small waves that break in thigh- or waist-deep water so you can push off the bottom to get momentum. The biggest push forward should be at the exact moment you feel the wave push against you. To catch the wave, your momentum must match that of the wave. If you push too soon, you will already be slowing when the wave catches up to you. And it will pass without taking you along. If you push off too late, the wave will have already passed you by.

Push forward with arms and body extended on the surface of the water, not above or below it. All of your movement should be forward, not up or down.

Pull your arms down to your side to generate some extra thrust and shape your body like a surfboard.

Face forward and roll your shoulders so they hug the surface of the water. Put your hands on your thighs. Lifting the head makes your feet drop. This slows you down and the wave passes you by.

Kick to maintain your speed if you have your fins on; keep your feet still and needle-like if you don't.

Feel the wave taking you with it. If you don't feel yourself being propelled with the wave, you missed it.

If the waves aren't pushing you along, it might be because they are too small or mushy, but it is probably because your timing isn't right yet.

Keep working on it; you will get catch on soon enough. The first time you actually ride a wave is a thrill. It is hard to describe the sensation, but you will know it when it happens.

Even if you never learn to ride a whole wave (from the beginning), knowing how to ride the whitewater is very useful on its own.

RIDE THE WHOLE WAVE

Once you have mastered the whitewater, you will be ready to catch waves from the beginning. Stick with small waves. The technique is the same as for riding whitewater, but you have to be in just the right spot to catch the waves. Since the waves are just starting to break, they will be further out in deeper water. This is where the fins will really help because you will probably have to swim to get momentum rather than pushing off the bottom (depending on how deep the water is). You can either adjust your position constantly (since no two waves will break at exactly the same spot) or wait for the right wave to come to you.

Predicting where waves will break takes time and experience so expect some difficulty. One trick is to stay near, but not in the way of, someone who seems to know what they are doing and watch how they time their take-off into the waves. As with riding whitewater, you need to push off at just the right time. The biggest difference is that when you ride a wave from the beginning (using the straight-in method), you drop vertically with the lip of the wave as it crashes. There is a moment of truth when you look down at the face of the wave opening up under you. At the last minute, you may hesitate and/or pull back in an escape attempt that is usually fruitless. The wave may pull you into it anyway in an awkward position and you will be pounded mercilessly. This is known as going over the falls and is discussed a bit more later.

It is crucial to maintain your surfboard-like form at this moment that is the scariest and also the fastest, most fun part of the ride. Practice on small waves and ride larger ones as your skill improves. Don't worry about learning to tuck out of the waves. For your purposes, you want to ride them as far as they will take you.

WAVE-RIDING ETIQUETTE

Learning this stuff is difficult enough without making the locals angry with you. Be aware of other wave riders and do your best to stay out of their way as they zip across the waves. Since you are trying to learn to ride the waves straight in while everyone else is riding across them, it is likely that at some point you will begin your straight in ride in front of someone else who is coming toward you across the wave. The rule is that the first one riding the wave gets it. So if someone is riding toward you on a wave, don't try to catch it. Don't worry yourself silly over it, but do be aware and try to be courteous.

SKILL #19: SIGHT BACKWARD

Danger always comes from the ocean, not the land. As you round the final buoy and approach the beach, you have to know if there are any waves coming up behind you. The last thing you want is to get blasted by a big wave that you never saw coming.

As you lift your elbow out of the water, glance behind and under your arm. It may take more than one stroke to get a clear view. If a wave is coming, decide if you want to try to ride it in. This is where all of your practice will pay off. If the wave is too big, let it pass by. If it is too small, you won't be able to catch it because it will break much closer to the beach. In any case, you have to be able to gauge your position relative to where the wave will break and act (speed up, slow, or dive under) accordingly.

Move fast once you are in the impact zone. If you don't ride the waves or the whitewater, then it is best to get to shore between the breaking waves. If the surge is strong, you may want to stand and start running through the water sooner than you would in a lake that has no current. The dolphin technique described in Chapter 9 is useful for exiting the water. Think of it as a speedy compromise between swimming and running but remember that the water is getting shallower as you go. Keep your hands in front of your head and don't dive too deep.

The movement of the water, the sighting forward and back, bodysurfing and dolphining can all make you extra woozy when you first stand up. Take a moment and steady yourself before you run up the beach.

SKILL #20: SURVIVING WIPEOUTS

Eventually it happens to everyone who goes into the surf, whether you are trying to bodysurf, go under waves or are just hanging around. To call it a skill may seem odd, but fearless swimmers handle wipeouts better than nervous beginners. Knowing how to handle a wipeout does wonders for your confidence. Anyone who has spent time in the surf has probably gone over the falls, even if you did not know what it was called. Indeed, such an experience is often what convinces people to give up on the surf permanently.

It starts with being drawn up and over the crest of the wave as it breaks. It is like going over a waterfall and that is how it is named. A moment of weightlessness is followed by a hefty impact that mashes you, draws you up again and shoves you around in every direction until you are completely disoriented and out of air. A bit more sloshing occurs, and when you feel like you are just about to drown, you find the bottom and push to the surface.

The ocean is a marvelous teacher. She will let you know when you have made a mistake. If you go over the falls, you either tried to catch a wave at the wrong moment, tried to escape when the wave already had you, or you didn't dive under a wave soon and deep enough. Learn the lesson and try again.

A bad wipeout might shake you up enough that you have to get out of the water to recover. The meek may return defeated to the safety of the pool, but as a fearless swimmer in training you will come to understand that wipeouts come with the territory. They are easier to handle when you stop being afraid of them. Waves crash and roll, and wipeouts are unstoppable once they begin. The best thing to do is to curl up a little, cover your head, relax and go along with it. Your goal should be to relax as much as possible so you conserve air. Indeed, if the waves are small, the whole thing can be sort of fun. With experience, you will come to see these mishaps as exercises in patience, not life or death struggles.

PUTTING IT ALL TOGETHER ON RACE DAY

If you have an ocean race coming up, it is important to see the swim venue beforehand. You can study the waves and identify potential hazards and imagine yourself having an enjoyable swim.

On race day, you should study the surfline so you know whether there are rocks waiting for you in the water. Figure out which way the current is flowing and how strong it is so you can position yourself well for the start. Look for riptides and decide if they will be useful to you.

Follow your usual warm-up routine. Wade into the water near the starting line and notice whether there are any inshore holes, rocks or other hazards that could hamper you. If you are not comfortable going past the waves for your warm-up, splash around in the shallows for a while and get your face wet. Then do some running along the beach to warm up your muscles and get your heart rate up.

When you line up for the start, you should be keenly focused on the incoming surf so you know what is coming. The dark lines you see are distant swells that will become waves. Prominent lines indicate bigger waves, but sometimes they are blurred by high winds.

If the gun sounds as an enormous set is approaching the beach, you will be tempted to dive right in like everyone else. But it might be better to wait for the biggest waves to pass. Swimming through a mountain of whitewater is a fruitless expense of energy. Don't be one of the athletes that gets pulled from the surf within five minutes of the start, exhausted and terrified. Time things so that your swimming will be productive. It is all right to wait a little before you go, even though the clock is ticking.

When the time is right, jog to about knee-deep water then either wade or begin dolphin diving to about mid-thigh depth to begin swimming. The adrenaline will be flowing, you will be looking for a spot among the swimmers around you, the current will be surging and there will be waves approaching, too. The key is to get out past the impact zone as quickly as possible. Use a riptide if one is handy.

Dolphin dive under and swim skillfully over the waves. If the buoy is not readily visible, just follow the other swimmers. Notice the rhythm on the swells and settle into your pace. As you round the final buoy and approach the beach, look behind you for incoming waves. Get through the impact zone quickly and enjoy the ride. When your hands touch bottom, stand up and run up the beach. Confidence and skill will rule the day.

Appendix

APPENDIX A:
SELF-ASSESSMENT FOR ANXIETY

This is the Sheenan Self-assessment Test for Anxiety (1). This test is based on the predominant symptoms of anxiety disorders as listed in the DSM IV. Please use the results of this test as a guide and not a diagnosis, as only a licensed mental health practitioner can diagnose anxiety disorders. The purpose of this test is to identify and measure the severity of symptoms associated with anxiety. It is useful for measuring a patient's progress.

Scoring: Assign a value of 0 to 4 to each question. At the end, score the total test. Symptom detected.....................................
0 = Not At All
1 = A Little
2 = Moderately
3 = Quite a Bit
4 = Extremely

1. Difficulty in getting your breath, smothering, or over breathing
2. Choking sensation or a lump in the throat
3. Skipping, racing, or pounding of your heart
4. Chest pain, pressure, or discomfort
5. Bouts of excessive sweating
6. Faintness, light-headedness, or dizzy spells
7. Sensation of rubbery or "jelly" legs
8. Feeling off-balance or unsteady like you might fall
9. Nausea or stomach problems
10. Feeling that things around you are strange, unreal, foggy, or detached from you
11. Feeling outside or detached from part or all of your body, or floating freely
12. Tingling or numbness in parts of your body
13. Hot flashes or cold chills
14. Shaking or trembling
15. Having a fear that you are dying or that something terrible is about to happen
16. Feeling you are losing control or going insane
17. Sudden anxiety attacks with three or more of the symptoms listed above that occur when you are in or are about to go into a situation that is likely, from your experience, to bring on an attack

18. Sudden unexpected anxiety attacks with three or more symptoms listed above that occur with little or no provocation (i.e., when you are NOT in a situation that is likely, from your experience, to bring on an attack)
19. Sudden unexpected spells with only one or two symptoms (listed above) that occur with little or no provocation (i.e., when you are NOT in a situation that is likely, from your experience, to bring on an attack)
20. Anxiety episodes that build up as you anticipate doing something that is likely, from your experience, to bring on anxiety that is more intense than most people experience in such situations
21. Avoiding situations because they frighten you
22. Being dependent on others
23. Tension and inability to relax
24. Anxiety, nervousness, restlessness
25. Spells of increased sensitivity to sound, light, or touch
26. Attacks of diarrhea
27. Worrying about your health too much
28. Feeling tired, weak, and/or exhausted easily
29. Headaches or pains in the neck or head
30. Difficulty in falling asleep
31. Waking in the middle of the night, or restless sleep
32. Unexpected waves of depression occurring with little or no provocation
33. Emotions and moods going up and down a lot in response to changes around you
34. Recurrent and persistent ideas, thoughts, impulses, or images that are intrusive, unwanted, senseless, or repugnant
35. Having to repeat the same action in a ritual, e.g., checking, washing, counting repeatedly, when it's not really necessary

Results:
Scores above 30 are usually considered abnormal, and scores above 80 are noted as severe. The mean score in panic disorder and agoraphobia is 57 (+/- 20). The goal of treatment is to bring the score below 20.

Disclaimer:
This is only a preliminary screening test for anxiety symptoms that does not replace in any way a formal psychiatric evaluation. It is designed to give a preliminary idea about the presence of mild to moderate anxiety symptoms that indicate the need for an evaluation by a psychiatrist.

APPENDIX B:
EVALUATING YOUR CARDIAC RISK

This risk assessment tool is widely available, but was provided with permission by Lawrence L. Creswell, M.D. from his blog, http://athletesheart.blogspot.com.

It's important to know your personal risk for the development of coronary heart disease (CHD) because the effectiveness of drugs (or other treatments) in preventing you from developing CHD depend very much on your inherent risk.

Over many decades, data have been collected by the Framingham study on a very large number of Americans about their health and lifestyle habits. One byproduct from this large database has been the development of equations that can be used to predict your 10-year risk of developing CHD.

Use the "worksheets" below to tally up points for your LDL score and your Chol score. When you've tallied up the points, you'll use the appropriate table to determine your 10-year risk of CHD. We need to consider men and women separately because the risks are different. Thus there are separate "worksheets" and tables for men and women. This is an important number, and you should talk about this with your doctor when you visit.

FOR MEN
Step 1: Age
30-34: LDL score = -1; Chol score = -1.
35-39: LDL score = 0; Chol score = 0.
40-44: LDL score = 1; Chol score = 1.
45-49: LDL score = 2; Chol score = 2.
50-54: LDL score = 3; Chol score = 3.
55-59: LDL score = 4; Chol score = 4.
60-64: LDL score = 5; Chol score = 5.
65-69: LDL score = 6; Chol score = 6.
70-74: LDL score = 7; Chol score = 7.

Step 2: Serum lipid levels
LDL cholesterol (mg/dL)
<100: LDL score = -3.
100-159: LDL score = 0.
160-190: LDL score = 1.
>=190: LDL score = 2.

Cholesterol (mg/dL)
<160: Chol score = -3.
160-199: Chol score = 0.
200-239: Chol score = 1.
240-279: Chol score = 2.
>=280: Chol score = 3.

HDL cholesterol (mg/dL)
<35: LDL score = 2; Chol score = 2.
35-44: LDL score = 1; Chol score = 1.
45-54: LDL score = 0; Chol score = 0.
>=55: LDL score = -1; Chol score = -2.

Step 3: Blood pressure
(check your score for systolic and diastolic blood pressures, but use ONLY the highest score, not both).

Systolic pressure (top number, mmHg)
<120: LDL score = 0; Chol score = 0.
120-129: LDL score = 0; Chol score = 0.
130-139: LDL score = 1; Chol score = 1.
140-159: LDL score = 2; Chol score = 2.
>=160: LDL score = 3; Chol score = 3.

Diastolic pressure (bottom number, mmHg)
<80: LDL score = 0; Chol score = 0.
80-84: LDL score = 0; Chol score = 0.
85-89: LDL score = 1; Chol score = 1.
90-99: LDL score = 2; Chol score = 2.
>=100: LDL score = 3; Chol score = 3.

Step 4: Do you have diabetes?
No: LDL score = 0; Chol score = 0.
Yes: LDL score = 2; Chol score = 2.

Step 5: Are you a smoker?
No: LDL score = 0; Chol score = 0
Yes: LDL score = 2; Chol score = 2

Tally your score and use the table below to determine your risk of developing CHD in the next 10 years.

FOR WOMEN
Step 1: Age
30-34: LDL score = -9; Chol score = -9.
35-39: LDL score = -4; Chol score = -4.
40-44: LDL score = 0; Chol score = 0.
45-49: LDL score = 3; Chol score = 3.
50-54: LDL score = 6; Chol score = 6.
55-59: LDL score = 7; Chol score = 7.
60-64: LDL score = 8; Chol score = 8.
65-69: LDL score = 8; Chol score = 8.
70-74: LDL score = 8; Chol score = 8.

Step 2: Serum lipid levels
LDL cholesterol (mg/dL)
<100: LDL score = -2.
100-159: LDL score = 0.
160-190: LDL score = 2.
>=190: LDL score = 2.

Cholesterol (mg/dL)
<160: Chol score = -2.
160-199: Chol score = 0.
200-239: Chol score = 1.
240-279: Chol score = 1.
>=280: Chol score = 3.

HDL cholesterol (mg/dL)
<35: LDL score = 5; Chol score = 5.
35-44: LDL score = 2; Chol score = 2.
45-49: LDL score = 1; Chol score = 1.
45-54: LDL score = 0; Chol score = 0.
>=55: LDL score = -2; Chol score = -3.

Step 3: Blood pressure
(check your score for systolic and diastolic blood pressures, but use ONLY the highest score, not both)

Systolic pressure (top number, mmHg)
<120: LDL score = -3; Chol score = -3.
120-129: LDL score = 0; Chol score = 0.
130-139: LDL score = 0; Chol score = 0.
140-159: LDL score = 2; Chol score = 2.
>=160: LDL score = 3; Chol score = 3.

Diastolic pressure (bottom number, mmHg)
<80: LDL score = -3; Chol score = -3.
80-84: LDL score = 0; Chol score = 0.
85-89: LDL score = 0; Chol score = 0.
90-99: LDL score = 2; Chol score = 2.
>=100: LDL score = 3; Chol score = 3.

Step 4: Do you have diabetes?
No: LDL score = 0; Chol score = 0.
Yes: LDL score = 4; Chol score = 4.

Step 5: Are you a smoker?
No: LDL score = 0; Chol score = 0.
Yes: LDL score = 2; Chol score = 2.

Tally your score and use the table below to determine your risk of developing CHD in the next 10 years.

APPENDIX C:
A TRIATHLETE'S GUIDE TO SWIMMING INDUCED PULMONARY EDEMA (SIPE)

Charles C. Miller, III, PhD

WHAT IS SIPE?

Triathletes occasionally report breathing problems in the swim that include 1) shortness of breath that seems out of proportion to the work being done, and 2) cough productive of copious amounts of pink, frothy, brown or blood-tinged sputum. In the absence of overt cardiac or pulmonary disease, this is the phenomenon known as swimming induced pulmonary edema (SIPE). SIPE is worrisome to triathletes, both because the symptoms are alarming and because physicians who are consulted in the aftermath often aren't familiar with the diagnosis and therefore can't account for what happened to the patient. The good news about SIPE is that, in general, episodes are self-limiting and do not appear to cause long-term harm once they have resolved. The bad news is that SIPE is potentially hazardous during an acute attack while the athlete is still in the water, so the actual attack should be taken seriously by the affected person and anyone attempting to assist a swimmer in trouble.

Pulmonary edema occurs when blood or blood components from the circulatory system leak across the capillaries of the lungs into the air spaces. This leakage generally occurs when the permeability of the capillary membranes is increased by some sort of molecular signal or by lung injury (termed non-cardiogenic) or when the heart fails to maintain appropriate pressure relationships in the pulmonary capillaries (cardiogenic). Swimming induced pulmonary edema is estimated to occur in approximately 1.4% of triathletes (Miller, et al, American Journal of Emergency Medicine), and appears to occur in generally healthy people. SIPE has also been reported in Navy SEALS, as well as in apnea divers and SCUBA divers. It is generally considered to be due to non-cardiogenic causes, though some recent evidence suggests that high blood pressure may play a role as well. Swimming induced pulmonary edema is believed to result from a "perfect storm" mix of ten potential risk factors. These are: 1) water immersion; 2) exertion; 3) cold water; 4) over-hydration; 5) pulmonary capillary trauma; 6) neurohumoral abnormalities; 7) position in the water; 8) use of a tight wetsuit; 9) diastolic cardiac dysfunction; and 10) blood thinning medications.

Water immersion causes extrinsic pressure on the body, which squeezes blood from the extremities into the central circulation system, including the heart and blood vessels of the lungs. Increased blood volume shifted into the chest from the extremities can lead to increased pressure gradients across the capillaries in the lungs (pulmonary capillaries). The pulmonary capillaries at their thinnest are membranes across which the blood and air spaces in the lungs exchange oxygen and other gases, and these membranes can be susceptible to leakage when pressure gradients across them become too great. The body normally has an extraordinary capacity to regulate the pressure in the lung circuit, but occasionally the compensatory functions are overwhelmed and leakage occurs.

Exertion increases cardiac output, increases stress on the pulmonary capillaries, and may intensify the effects of any underlying issues, such as high blood pressure, decreased cardiac diastolic function, or other causes of capillary integrity loss.

Cold temperature exposure causes the peripheral capillaries to constrict, decreasing their volume and therefore their capacity to hold blood. In this way, the peripheral circulation forces blood volume from the extremities into the central circulation system in an attempt to maintain warmth. Significant heat loss is possible through the peripheral circulation when it is exposed to cold, and sequestration of the blood in the central circulation helps to conserve heat. In theory, this effect could work as a multiplier with the extrinsic water pressure to cause a major central blood volume shift, which again places stress on the heart and on pulmonary capillary transmural pressure gradients.

Over-hydration, which many athletes are conditioned to accomplish prior to competition, expands the volume of the plasma, which is the liquid component of the blood. Expanded plasma volume can make oxygen transport more efficient, which is why athletes like to do it, but when peripheral volume capacity shrinks due to extrinsic compression from water and wetsuits, and from internal capillary volume regulation in response to cold, the increased central volume becomes a larger burden for the central circulation to manage and can further stress the heart's capacity to pump and the amount of pressure the pulmonary capillaries can contain.

Direct trauma to the lung capillaries can occur with long-term hard exercise. Racehorses famously get pulmonary edema during heavy exercise, as their cardiac output overwhelms the ability of their pulmonary capillaries to manage the pressure. Racehorses are bred specifically to have hearts too large for their bodies in order to maximize their performance, as the heart is the engine of the endurance athlete. Like too big an engine in too small a car, the search for power is not consequence-free in racehorses. Human athletes fortunately are not bred for performance, but many top competitors naturally self-select for high cardiac output, and training also increases cardiac performance. Repeated high-stress training may cause physical shear stress trauma to the capillaries and may also contribute to free radical injury or other insults to the capillary membranes themselves. The cases that have been described in Navy SEALS and similar combat swimmers often occur in prolonged training, when hard swims follow long hours of stressful dry land endurance work. This temporal association is consistent with some role for capillary stress failure in such situations. Given that military Special Forces recruits are heavily screened for physical capability, these are likely to be extremely healthy people without underlying predisposing chronic risk factors. Triathletes, and especially long-course triathletes, may spend 20 or more hours per week training in the months prior to an event, and this would be expected to contribute to capillary stress failure risk.

Neurohumoral abnormalities can cause pulmonary edema. High altitude pulmonary edema, though poorly understood, is thought to result in part from neurohumoral abnormalities. The neurohumoral system refers to the group of physiological functions that regulates hormones such as adrenaline (epinephrine), which influence the function of the cardiovascular system. Neurohumoral activity can affect permeability of the vascular system including the capillaries, which can affect the strength of heart contractions and influence blood pressure by regulating vascular tone and the interaction of heart pumping with blood vessel response. The observation by some triathletes that a stressful swim start and the "adrenaline rush" that goes with it can trigger a SIPE episode is consistent with the hypothesis that neurohumoral factors could contribute to the development of swimming induced pulmonary edema.

Several of the studies conducted in military populations have implicated position in the water as a potential factor. Many Special Forces operatives swim in pairs and swim sidestroke to maintain visual contact. Several cases of edema have been reported in the dependent lung (the one on the deeper side) in this setting. Other cases have developed in combat swimmers who swim backward in a semi-seated position wearing large fins. Since the legs have a significant capacity to hold blood, some authors have suggested that the semi-seated position with the legs deeper than the trunk may favor increased hydrostatic pressure on the legs and consequently greater pressure return to the chest from the leg circulation. In triathletes, this is likely to be less of an issue. However, many coaches advise swimmers who get tired or freaked out by the swim to roll over on their backs to rest. How a change in swim posture due to rollover might affect a developing SIPE episode is unclear at the present time.

Wetsuits have been implicated anecdotally in SIPE, with several people who've had repeat episodes mentioning that wearing a wetsuit or changes in wetsuit fit might be contributors. The one study that has investigated this analytically as part of a survey was unable to separate wetsuit use from long course distance. Many Ironman distance events are wetsuit-eligible, and swimmers wear them for their buoyancy advantages in addition to their warmth. In a long swim, a wetsuit can be a significant advantage, particularly for less skilled swimmers, so most athletes wear them when possible. Without an experimental trial, it's very difficult to tell what the independent contribution of wetsuits to SIPE risk is. If wetsuits do contribute to SIPE formation, it would likely be by a similar mechanism to immersion and cold – by limiting the vascular capacitance of the extremities through application of external force. That is, squeezing the blood from the arms and legs (especially the legs) into the central circulation system. Multiplier effects with immersion and cold could also contribute.

Diastolic cardiac dysfunction refers to a decreased ability of the heart's left ventricle to fill properly between the beats that result in systolic ejection. In many cases, the wall of the left ventricular chamber is stiffened by a chronic condition like high blood pressure or diabetes (especially type 1 diabetes). A stiff ventricular wall has an impaired ability to relax enough to allow efficient filling, and this affects the pressures in the ventricle and also the pressure upstream of the ventricle in the pulmonary circulation. The blood that fills the left side of the heart is freshly oxygenated blood coming from the lungs. If the ventricle can't fill properly, blood regurgitates into the left atrium and increases the pressure inside the pulmonary circulation, which in turn pressurizes the pulmonary capillaries. If the pressure goes high enough, the capillaries start to leak and fluid crosses into the airspaces, where it is coughed up as pulmonary edema. Some thickening of the left heart muscle is a normal adaptation to endurance training, but the thickened ventricle of an athlete usually remains highly compliant and is not unduly prone to diastolic filling errors. Whether training adaptations might interact with a natively stiff ventricle that results from longstanding high blood pressure or diabetes is currently unknown. At least one study has shown that having high blood pressure is associated with a nearly five-fold increase in the odds of having a SIPE episode. This supports the diastolic dysfunction hypothesis.

Blood thinning medications have also been implicated as potential risk factors for SIPE. Studies of apnea divers have indicated that some of the divers who had SIPE episodes had taken aspirin prior their dives. Aspirin is believed in some diving circles to prevent decompression sickness, though to the best of my knowledge no data support this use. We found an increased association between SIPE symptoms and fish oil use in our recent survey. It's possible that blood thinning medications, or compounds with antiplatelet effects, might make it easier for blood to cross the pulmonary capillary membranes, but this risk is largely theoretical. More study of the potential for such effects is needed.

PREVENTION

The vast majority of triathletes will never have an episode of SIPE, as it is estimated to occur in only 1.4% of triathlon swimmers. Consequently, most triathletes will never have to worry about SIPE, and attempts to reduce risk for these athletes are not sensible. Those of us who have had one or more episodes of SIPE can take some comfort in the fact that attacks are unlikely to be caused by any single factor, and rather likely require a constellation of factors to set up a "perfect storm." Therefore, correction of just a few risk factors should likely be sufficient to control episodes. For someone who's had a prior SIPE episode, a prevention plan ought to be discussed with a doctor, and whether or not to return to competition should be weighed in the context of competent medical advice (which is not conveyed by this article).

The most obvious preventative strategies are to avoid over-hydration prior to the swim and to treat any underlying conditions, such as high blood pressure or diabetes. Moderate hydration prior to the swim is adequate – any deficit coming out of the water will be small and can be made up on the bike.

Athletes with severe high blood pressure or type 1 diabetes should consult their physicians prior to undertaking a major triathlon preparation effort. For mild to moderate high blood pressure that isn't adequately controlled by exercise and salt intake restriction alone, angiotensin-converting enzyme II (ACE II) inhibitors, such as losartan, have been shown to improve ventricular relaxation, and there are good reasons to believe that this class of medications may be helpful in reducing SIPE risk. We have had anecdotal reports of hypertensive triathletes who have reduced or eliminated their SIPE episodes via treatment with ACE II inhibitors. ACE inhibitors are generally a better choice for athletes than beta blockers or diuretics, which are often prescribed for mild hypertension, because ACE II inhibitors have less potential to limit performance.

HOW TO TELL IF AN ATTACK IS OCCURRING

SIPE may come on rapidly or slowly, but it usually presents as a sensation of shortness of breath that is out of proportion to the effort being expended, a rattling sensation with breathing or a feeling of junk or phlegm in the lungs, and most obviously, a profound cough that produces copious amounts of sputum that may be pink, frothy, brown or blood-tinged. SIPE is distinct from exercise-induced asthma (or any kind of asthma for that matter), in that asthma is characterized mainly by wheezing, tightness in the airways, and an impaired ability to blow air out of the lungs. Any sputum produced by asthma should not be pink or bloody. Most people report SIPE within the first 15-20 minutes of a swim, although it can start later in very long events. A swimmer who has a sudden onset of shortness of breath that is unfamiliar, especially if it is accompanied by a productive cough, should spit out what he or she is coughing up and get a look at it. If it's pink, frothy or bloody, it's pulmonary edema. Of particular note is that SIPE only occurs during immersion. On rare occasions, athletes will develop pulmonary edema during the bike or the run, but this is usually due to an underlying condition, such as significant high blood pressure (flash pulmonary edema), acute myocardial infarction (heart attack) or a cardiac structural defect, like a patent foramen ovale or other communication between the left and right sides of the heart. Pulmonary edema that occurs on dry land is quite serious and is not SIPE. Dry land pulmonary edema requires immediate medical attention.

WHAT TO DO IF A SIPE EPISODE OCCURS

An athlete who experiences an episode of SIPE should get out of the water immediately. The attack will not subside as long as the person remains underwater, so the first line of treatment is extraction. In general, SIPE is self-limiting once the person gets out of the water and calms down, though in some cases supplemental oxygen and diuretics may be indicated. Pulse oximetry is helpful if for no other reason that it's reassuring to the medical staff and to the patient, and of course it can help to guide therapy as necessary. Athletes, and especially ultra-endurance athletes, are a hard-driven bunch, and many of them will want to get back in the game as soon as the episode resolves. In a sport that involves navigating a crowded bike course and a demanding run, this is not a good idea. SIPE should end the day's performance and lead to a follow-up visit with a physician who is familiar with the problem. There exists the possibility that a SIPE episode could be significant enough to cause consciousness-altering hypoxia. A swim monitor who sees a swimmer coughing heavily or rolling over onto his or her back repeatedly (or both coughing and rolling over) should go over and take a look, then engage the swimmer in a conversation adequate to judge the swimmer's mental status.

LIKELY AFTERMATH

Several follow-up studies in directly observed SIPE cases in military populations have not demonstrated any harm or lingering effects. Cardiac and pulmonary function measures return to normal within a few weeks. This is not to say that SIPE is totally benign, however, because pulmonary edema-related deaths have been reported in divers. SIPE should be taken seriously but should not lead to panic. People with normal blood pressure who have never had an episode are at very low risk, likely 1% or less, and should not be worried about SIPE.

When an episode does occur, it should lead to an immediate exit from the water and a visit to the medical tent if it happens at a race. A follow-up consultation with a knowledgeable physician would be a good idea after the acute episode is controlled. An athlete should not be surprised if most personal physicians consulted afterward are not familiar with SIPE. We have received numerous reports of patients who have been admitted to ICU for observation, received CT scans, etc. when physicians haven't known what they were dealing with. A good consultation is most likely to be had with a sports-oriented cardiologist or sports medicine fellowship trained family physician. We know of several athletes who manage their SIPE effectively with medication, a good warm-up and avoidance of over-hydration. A SIPE episode should not be the end of a triathlete's career, but the decision to continue competition afterwards is a personal one that should be made in the context of advice from a competent physician.

Charles C. Miller, III, PhD, is an epidemiologist who works primarily in cardiovascular disease. He is Chair of the Department of Biomedical Sciences, Associate Dean for Research and Associate Dean for the Graduate School of Biomedical Sciences at the Texas Tech Paul L. Foster School of Medicine in El Paso, Texas. Dr. Miller had a SIPE episode in 2001.

APPENDIX D:
SUMMARY OF TRIATHLETE DEATHS

Here is a brief description of the sequence of events that claimed the lives of fellow triathletes during the swim portion of races. If I have excluded any, it is not intentional. I attempted to find witness accounts but for some victims there was very little information available.

The summaries emphasize events leading to the death, rather than specifics about the victims.

BARNETT GRIFFIN

Dorothy Barnett Griffin, age 43, died during the swim at Ironman Florida 2006. It was her first Ironman. No autopsy was done. She was one of the last two swimmers in the water and had stopped and chatted with volunteers on kayaks and paddlers several times. She was out of breath but positive about continuing. One source reported that she had a volunteer escorting her in the last part of the race. She apparently rolled onto her back, said "help" and became unconscious. She was immediately pulled from the water. Cause of death was not determined (1, 39).

BOLAND

John H. Boland, age 53, drowned in the now notorious Utah Lake "chaos swim" of the 2002 Ironman, where wind gusts of 30 mph produced 3-foot waves that capsized boats and tore buoys from their moorings. Boland had done two previous Ironman races. An autopsy was performed, but the cause of death was not disclosed. Boland was the first athlete to die in a triathlon swim (2).

COULSTON

Phillip Coulston, 63, died 100 yards from the finish of the 1.5-mile swim leg of the Escape From The Rock Triathlon on August 24, 2008. His son-in-law, who was swimming with him for moral support, led the efforts to revive him. Coulston had no history of heart problems. Witnesses said, "He kept resting. He would swim for a while, and then he would roll over and rest." "He rolled over to rest, and just stopped breathing" (3).

EIMERMAN

Daniel Eimerman, age 55, died at the Devil's Challenge Triathlon in 2007. He had atherosclerotic disease. Other participants noticed him moving slowly on his back during the race on Saturday morning. Witnesses say that they had asked him in the water if he was OK and he had said "yes" (4).

Lifeguards went toward Eimermann and quickly found that he was unconscious. He was given CPR and taken the hospital where he was pronounced dead.

FINDLAY

Patrick Findlay, 45, died of a heart attack during the Pacific Crest Triathlon in June 2009. Witnesses report that he swam to a volunteer boat and asked for help. He lost consciousness before the crew could pull him in. Findlay was a fit, seasoned triathlete (5, 6).

GOODMAN

Jim Goodman died at the Iowa Hy-Vee Triathlon in June of 2008. He was 46 years old, and this was his second triathlon. He signaled for help when he was about 150 meters from the shore of Blue Heron Lake. Rescuers in a nearby boat immediately jumped into the water, pulled Goodman out and began resuscitation efforts. He had a previously undetected heart condition (7). Witnesses said, "He signaled for help, so he knew he was in distress. ... He knew he was in trouble. He was able to talk" (8).

HOBGOOD

John Hobgood, Jr., age 52, died at his first triathlon, the New Jersey State Tri in July 2008. He had trained well and was an avid cyclist. He never exited the water. Officials searched for hours then called it off at 8pm due to weather and darkness. The family held an overnight vigil and at 1am discovered the body. An autopsy ruled the cause of death as accidental drowning (9).

HUNT

In June 2007, Kevin Hunt died at Austin Lake in his first triathlon. Hunt, 28, sank and drowned 50 feet from finishing the 500-yard swim. „The medical examiner said Kevin was as healthy as a horse. There was nothing wrong with his heart, and the toxicology report came back negative" (10).

Witnesses observed him yell for help twice before he went under (11). It took rescue personnel several minutes to locate him.

JARIN

On September 6 2009, Lor Porciuncula Jarin, 51, died during the swim of the Mount Shasta Tinman Triathlon at Lake Siskiyou (24). Anoxia (lack of oxygen) and pulmonary hemorrhage (bleeding from the lung) were listed as causes of death (25).

Jarin had completed the first half of the swim and was returning to the marina when spectators on the dock heard him calling for help. A witness said, "He made it to the rope and was holding the rope." He had rolled onto his back. People on the dock began yelling for help and waving their arms to signal for the rescue boat, as two other swimmers attempted to hold Jarin's head above water until the boat arrived (38).

KANE

Patrick Kane, age 38, died in May 2008 at the Gulf Coast Tri (70.3 distance, which he had done the year before as well). No autopsy was done, and the cause of death is indicated as accidental drowning. Newspapers reported that Kane flipped over during the 1.2-mile swimming leg of the competition and was then pulled from the water (12).

LYONS

Joseph J. Lyons died in July 2007 at the Cohasset Sprint Triathlon. He was 38. Less than 30 minutes into the swim, swimmers noticed him struggling in the water. He suffered a heart attack (13).

MARSHALL

Juli Wilson Marshall, 48, was pulled unconscious from the water of Tampa Bay during the St. Anthony's Triathlon in St. Petersburg in May 2007. The Olympic distance race had 4,000 entrants (14). Cause of death following autopsy was listed as "complications of drowning" (15).

MOREHOUSE

At the Spudman Triathlon in 2008, a very fit Donald Morehouse, age 60, was seen waving and calling for help by several witnesses, before he slipped beneath the surface. Despite a quick response, it took divers 20-30 minutes to find his body 10 feet underwater (16).

MURRY

Daniel Murry died during the Pewaukee Triathlon in July 2009. He was 33 years old. Murray had lost 100 lbs. from a lifetime high of 300 lbs., and this was his first triathlon. Witnesses said, "He grabbed onto the lifeguard boat on the first turn. He was there for a short period of time. He was resting for a while." He was seen grabbing a flotation device, then lost consciousness and slipped underwater. The family said he had a history of heart problems. Daniel died early in the swim (17, 18, 19).

NIERA

Esteban Niera, age 32, died at the New York City Triathlon in July 2008. He was pulled unconscious from the water. Cause of death was hypertensive cardiovascular disease. Niera was apparently unaware of his condition (20).

PARNELL

51-year-old Randolph Parnell had been doing triathlons for 11 years when he died at the CB & I Triathlon at Lake Woodlands in May 2008. He died after swimming in the first leg of the triathlon. He was an experienced athlete in excellent health, a family member said. Yet, minutes after telling a lifeguard that he was doing OK during the 500-meter swim. He was found floating face down (21).

PIEW

In October of 2005, 40 year-old Ho Wai Piew died during the swim leg of the New Balance Corporate Triathlon in Singapore. It was his first triathlon. The cause of death was certified as drowning, heart attack and advanced coronary arterial disease (22, 23).

RICE

Barney Rice died at Ironman Florida in 2006. He was 35 years old, and on his second lap of the choppy swim. He was rounding the far buoy. A participant ran into Rice's body and signaled for help. Rescue personnel got to him within 30 seconds and brought him to the beach on a sled, performing chest compressions the whole way.

The autopsy ruled drowning as cause of death. Rice had no pre-existing conditions. Rice said earlier his goal was simply to finish and "stay calm on the swim." Rice died of a massive heart attack (26, 27, 28).

SCHMIDT

43 year-old Kim Schmidt died at the Oshkosh Triathlon in 2009. It was her first triathlon. Reports say that early on it was clear something was wrong with Schmidt. Witnesses saw her swimming slowly near the park, and she stopped to hold on to a buoy. "A lifeguard went in immediately and found her and said, 'Are you OK?' and she said, 'Yes, I'm OK. But is it OK to do the backstroke?' and she said, "yes, that's fine," so she went on to her back and started doing the backstroke." Another swimmer heard Schmidt wheezing and alerted the lifeguards (29).

SILLETTI

In August 2009, Julie Silletti, 54, was doing backstroke as she finished the 400m swim of the Elkhart Lake Triathlon, her first outdoor race. She stood up, looked tired, and complained of chest pain. Lifeguards helped her to shore where she collapsed (30).

SIMPSON

Paul Simpson died as a result of a sudden and unexpected cardiac arrest during the swimming leg of The London Olympic Distance triathlon on August 5, 2006 (31).

SING

Calvin Lee Wee Sing, age 42, died in August 2009 at the OSIM Singapore Triathlon. He was the most fit member of the relay team and was found disoriented and foaming at the mouth. He was a strong swimmer but appeared to be struggling and disoriented in the water about 350m from the finish line of the 1.5km swim race. He was rescued quickly but could not be resuscitated (32).

VASQUEZ

52-year-old Miguel Vasquez, who died during the first Cobra Ironman Philippines in Cam Sur in 2009, was a "strong swimmer" according to friends. He worked out regularly with a personal trainer at the Manila Polo Club but suffered a stroke in the waters of Lago Del Ray (33).

VEITH

Michael David Veith died in 2003 while swimming in a triathlon near his Spokane home. Veith, 57, was a master swimmer on a relay team that set a national age record two years ago. He drowned 125 yards short of the finish in the 1.2-mile swimming leg of the Troika Triathlon. A kayak support boat pulled him ashore, but medics could not revive him (34). Later reports were that he died of hyperthermia (overheating) because of his wetsuit (35).

WIWCHAR

At Ironman Canada in 2009, Walter Eugene (Wally) Wiwchar, age 66, drowned as the result of a heart condition (dissection of his aorta). Although Wiwchar was participating in his first full Ironman, he had finished half-Ironman and shorter races. A witness saw him raise his hands to signal for assistance (36). Lifeguards spotted him struggling on the final leg of the triangular course. Observers said he headed off course, away from most of the other swimmers. He was attended to by an escort kayaker and given immediate attention (37).

APPENDIX E:
RACE DAY TROUBLESHOOTING

Below are some quick tips for race day.

1. Avoid caffeine on race day.
2. Slow belly breathing will calm you down.
3. Swim at a slower pace-make an opposite time goal: "I will swim no faster than_____ "
4. Focus on your hands in murky water.
5. Ask lifeguards to keep a special eye on you.
6. Count strokes.
7. Use positive self-talk.
8. Use wide-angle goggles if you are prone to motion sickness.
9. Find humor in what you are doing.
10. Have patience.
11. Avoid water vehicles that produce fumes.
12. Float on your back when you feel claustrophobic.
13. Don't wear a wetsuit unless you are 100% comfortable in it.
14. Sing a song in your mind as you swim.
15. Switch to an easier stroke – breaststroke, sidestroke, backstroke are all OK during races.
16. Rest on a paddleboard.
17. Wear earplugs to minimize cold water in the ear, which causes dizziness.
18. Tuck a whistle into your cap. Blow it if you get into trouble.
19. Start on the far edge of the group of athletes at the starting line.
20. Delay your start by 20 seconds to let the mob get ahead of you.
21. Don't race with a fever or if you feel poorly.
22. Get help immediately if you have unusual sensations during the swim.
23. Find large landmarks for sighting.
24. Warm up long enough to normalize your heart rate.
25. Get your face and neck wet before going in the water all the way.
26. Pre-warm your wetsuit if the water is exceptionally cold.
27. At the finish, walk out of the water, don't run.

REFERENCES

Section 1:
Chapter 1: **How to Become a Fearless Swimmer**
(1) Grand' Maison, K. (2004). What mental skills Ironman triathletes need and want. Journal of Excellence. Issue 10. Retreived May 2010, from http://www.Zoneofexcellence.com.
(2) Anxietypanic.com. Anxiety and Panic Attacks. Retrieved March 2010, from http://www.anxietypanic.com.
(3) Cox, L. (2004). Swimming To Antarctica: Tales of a Long Distance Swimmer. Harvest Books, pp. 28-29.

Chapter 2: **Mental Tools**
(1) Heller, S. (1999). Complete Idiot's Guide to Conquering Fear and Anxiety. Penguin Group.
(2) Bernardi, L., Porta, C., Gabutti, A., Spicuzza, L. & Sleight, P. (2001). Modulatory effects of respiration. Autonomic Neuroscience, 90(1-2), 47-56.
(3) Sang, Y.P., Fleur, D., Golding, J.F. & Gresty, M.A. (2003). Suppression of sickness by controlled breathing during mildly nauseogenic motion. Aviation, Space, and Environmental Medicine, 74(9), 998-1002.
(4) Simons, D. (2000). Attentional capture and inattentional blindness. Trends in Cognitive Sciences, 4(4),147-155.
(5) Schiller, D., Levy, I., Niv, Y., LeDoux, J.E., & Phelps, E.A. (2008). From fear to safety and back: reversal of fear in the human brain. Journal of Neuroscience, 28(45), 11517-25.
(6) Marks, I. (1987). Fears, Phobias and Rituals: Panic, Anxiety and Their Disorders. Oxford University Press, p. 344.

Chapter 3: **Solve Annoying Problems**
(1) Long, L., Horn, M., Stofan, J., Horsewill, C.A. & Murray, R. (2001). Induction of localized leg cramps using a run/swim protocol: A pilot study. Medicine & Science in Sports & Exercise, 33(5), S325.
(2) Sulzer, N.U., Schwellnus, M.P. & Noakes, T.D. (2005). Serum electrolytes in Ironman triathletes with exercise-associated muscle cramping. Medicine & Science in Sports & Exercise, 37(7), 1081-5.
(3) Schwellnus, M.P. (2007). Muscle cramping in the marathon : Aetiology and risk factors. Sports Medicine, 37(4-5), 364-7.
(4) Maquirriain, J. & Merello, M. (2007). The athlete with muscular cramps: Clinical approach. Journal of the American Academy of Orthopaedic Surgeons, 15(7), 425-31.
(5) Schwellnus, M.P. (2009). Cause of Exercise Associated Muscle Cramps(EAMC) altered neuromuscular control, dehydration or electrolyte depletion. British Journal of Sports Medicine. 43(6), 401-408.
(6) Schwellnus, M.P., Drew, N. & Collins, M. (2008). Muscle cramping in athletes—risk factors, clinical assessment, and management. Clinics in Sports Medicine, 27(1), 183-94.
(7) Hew-Butler, T.D., Sharwood, K., Collins, M., Speedy, D. & Noakes, T. (2006). Sodium supplementation is not required to maintain serum sodium concentrations during an Ironman triathlon. British Journal of Sports Medicine, 40(3), 255-9.

(8) Hiller, W.D.B., O'Toole, M., Fortess, E.E., Laird, R.H., Imbert, P.C. & Sisk, T.D. (1987). Medical and physiological considerations in triathlon. American Journal of Sports Medicine, 15(2), 164-167.

(9) Yanofsky, C. & Lemoyne, P.A. http://www.pneuro.com. (retreived February 2010).

(10) Cheung, B.S., Money, K.E. & Jacobs, I. (1990). Motion sickness susceptibility and aerobic fitness: A longitudinal study. Aviation, Space, and Environmental Medicine, 61(3):201-4.

(11) Reavley, C.M., Golding, J.F., Cherkas, L.F., Spector, T.D. & MacGregor, A.J. (2006).Genetic influences on motion sickness susceptibility in adult women: a classical twin study. Aviation, Space and Environmental Medicine. 77(11), 1148-52.

(12) Ishii, C., Nishino, L.K. & Herrerias de Campos, C.A. (2009). Vestibular characterization in the menstrual cycle. Brazilian Journal of Otorhinolarynology, 75(3), 375-80.

(13) Golding, J.F., Kadzere, P. & Gresty, M.A. (2005). Motion sickness susceptibility fluctuates through the menstrual cycle. Aviation, Space, and Environmental Medicine, 76(10):970-3.

(14) Pascoe, D. Carbon Monoxide Alert. (1999, June 30). Carbon monoxide alert. Boat Handling & Boat Safety. Retrieved March 2010 from
http://www.yachtsurvey.com/carbon_monoxide_alert.htm.

(15) Haber, A. (2010). A Guide to Prevent Carbon Monoxide Poisoning. Retrieved March 2010 from http://www.carbon-monoxide-poisoning.com/article4-carbon-monoxide-boating.html .

(16) Sang, Y.P., Fleur, D., Golding, J. & Gresty, M.A. (2003). Suppression of sickness by controlled breathing during mildly nauseogenic motion . Aviation, Space, and Environmental Medicine, 74(9): 998-1002.

(17) Weinfuss, J. (2008, August 12). Tri-accidental tragedy Part II: Gulf risks threaten swimmers. News Herald. Retrieved from
http://www.newsherald.com/sports/gulf-67414-people-saltwater.html .

(18) Lien, H.C., Sun, W.M., Chen, Y.H., Kim, H., Hasler, W. & Owyang, C. (1984). Effects of ginger on motion sickness and gastric slow-wave dysrhythmias induced by circular vection. American Journal of Physiology – Gastrointestinal and Liver Physiology, 284(3), G481-9.

(19) Lee, A. & Fan, L.T.Y. (2009). Stimulation of the wrist acupuncture point P6 for preventing postoperative nausea and vomiting. Cochrane Database Syst Rev. 2, (CD003281).

(20) Taspinar, A. & Sirin, A. (2010) Effect of acupressure on chemotherapy-induced nausea and vomiting in gynecologic cancer patients in Turkey. European Journal of Oncology Nursing, 14(1), 49-54.

(21) Molassiotis, A., Helin, A.M., Dabbour, R. & Hummerston, S. (2007). The effects of P6 acupressure in the prophylaxis of chemotherapy-related nausea and vomiting in breast cancer patients.
Complementary Therapies in Medicine, 15(1), 3-12.

(22) Hain, T.C., Fuller, L., Weil, L. & Kotsias, J. (1999) Effects of T'ai Chi on Balance..Archives of Otolaryngology – Head & Neck Surgery, 125, 1191-1195.

(23) Caillet, G., Bosser, G., Gouchard, G.C., Chau, N., Benamghar, L. & Perrin, P.P. (2006). Effect of sporting activity practice on susceptibility to motion sickness. Brain Research Bulletin, 69(3), 288-93.

(24) Benson, AJ.(1999) Motion sickness. In: Aviation Medicine, 3rd edition, edited by Ernsting J. Nichloson, et al. Oxford Butterworth-Heinmann. P 455-61.

(25) Yen Pick Sang, F., Billar, J., Gresty, M.A. & Golding, J.F. (2005). Effect of a novel motion desensitization training regime and controlled breathing on habituation to motion sickness. Perceptual and Motor Skills, 101(1), 244-56.

(26) Clément, G., Deguine, O., Bourg, M. & Pavy-LeTraon, A. (2007). Effects of vestibular training on motion sickness, nystagmus, and subjective vertical . Journal of Vestibular Research, 17(5-6), 227-37.

(27) Yen Pick Sang, F., Billar, J., Gresty, M.A. & Golding, J.F. (2005). Effect of a novel motion desensitization training regime and controlled breathing on habituation to motion sickness. Percept Mot Skills. 101(1):244-56.

(28) Anonymous. (n.d.). Doctors' answers to "Frequently Asked Questions" – Sea sickness. Drug Infonet.com. Retrieved March 2010 from
http://www.druginfonet.com/index.php?pageID=faq/new/DISEASE_FAQ/Sea_Sickness.htm.

(29) van Marion, W.F., Bongaerts, M.C., Christiaanse, .JC., Hofkamp, H.G.& van Ouwerkerk, W. (1985). Influence of transdermal scopolamine on motion sickness during 7 days' exposure to heavy seas. Clinical Pharmacology & Therapeutics, 38(3), 301-5.

Chapter 4: Worst Case Scenarios-Triathlon Swimming Deaths

(1) Harris, K., Henry, J. & Rohman, E. (2010). Sudden death during the triathlon. Journal of the American Medical Association, 303(13), 1255-57.

(2) Munatones, S. USA Swimming National Open Water Swimming Team coach, writer, commentator.
Websites: www.dailynewsof openwaterswimming.com and www.10kswim.com.

(3) Katsouras, G., Sakabe, M., Comtois, P., Maguy, A., Burstein, B., Guerra, P.G., Talajic, M., & Nattel, S. (2009). Differences in atrial fibrillation properties under Vagal nerve stimulation versus atrial tachycardia remodeling, Heart Rhythm, 6(10), 1465-72.

(4) Ladich, E., Virmani, R. & Burke, A. (2006.) Sudden cardiac death not related to coronary atherosclerosis. Toxic Pathology, 34(1), 52-57.

(5) Carlson, T. (2009, July 1). Torbjorn Sindballe Q & A: Part 1. Slowtwitch.com. Retrieved March 2010 from http://www.slowtwitch.com/Interview/Torbjorn_Sindballe_Q_A_Part_1_895.html.

General Sources:

MacHose, M. & Peper, E. (1991). The effect of clothing on inhalation volume. Applied Psychophysiology and Biofeedback, 16(3), 261-5.

Anonymous. (n.d.). Sudden cardiac death. American Heart Association. Retrieved June 2010 from http://www.americanheart.org/presenter.jhtml?identifier=4741.

Chapter 5: Don't Ignore Your Heart

(1) Stephens, S. (2010). From Michelin Man to Iron Man. Heart Insight, 4(1), 11-13.

(2) Heidbüchel, H., Anné, W., Willems, R., Adriaenssens, B., Van de Werf, F. & Ector, H. (2006). Endurance sports is a risk factor for atrial fibrillation after ablation for atrial flutter. International Journal of Cardiology, 107(1), 67-72.

(3) Anonymous(n.d.)Cleveland Clinic. "What are the dangers of atrial fibrillation?" Retrieved October 2010 from http://my.clevelandclinic.org/heart/atrial_fibrillation/afib.aspx

(4) Hoogsteen, J., Schep, G., van Hemel, N.M. & van der Wall, E.E. (2004). Paroxysmal atrial fibrillation in male endurance athletes. A 9-year follow-up. Europace, 6(3), 222-8.

(5) Mont, l., Elosua, R. & Brugada, J. (2009). Endurance sport practice as a risk factor for atrial fibrillation and atrial flutter. Europace, 11(1), 11–17.

(6) Molina, L., Mont, L., Marrugat, J., Berruezo, A., Brugada, J., Bruguera, J., Rebato, C. & Elosua, R. (2008). Long-term endurance sport practice increases the incidence of lone atrial fibrillation in men: A follow-up study. Europace, 10(5), 618-623.

(7) Guasch, E., & Mont, L. (2010). Endurance sport practice and arrhythmias. In R. Brugada (Ed.), Clinical Approach to Sudden Cardiac Death Syndromes (pp. 57-72). Springer-Verlag London Limited.

(8) Fagard, R., Aubert, A., Lysens, R., Staessen, J., Vanhees, L. & Ameray, A. (1983). Noninvasive assessment of seasonal variations in cardiac structure and function in cyclists. Circulation, 67(4), 896-901.

(9) Pelliccia, A., Maron, B.J., De Luca, R., di Paolo, F. M., Spataro, A. & Culasso, F. (2002). Remodeling of left ventricular hypertrophy in elite athletes after long-term deconditioning. Circulation, 105(8), 944-949.

(10) McKelvie, R. (2009). Athlete's heart. The Merck Manuals Online Medical Library. Retrieved June 2010 from
http://www.merck.com/mmpe/sec07/ch082/ch082c.html#CIHCEGIE.

(11) Varró, A. & Baczkó, I. (2010). Possible mechanisms of sudden cardiac death in top athletes: a basic cardiac electrophysiological point of view. Pflugers Archive: European Journal of Physiology, 460(1), 31-40.

(12) Maron, B. J. (2005). Distinguishing hypertrophic cardiomyopathy from athlete's heart: A clinical problem of increasing magnitude and significance. Heart, 90, 1380-1382.

(13) Frick, M., Pachinger, O. & Pölzl, G. (2009). Myocarditis and sudden cardiac death in athletes. Diagnosis, treatment, and prevention. Herz, 34(4), 299-304.

(14) Harrison, A. M. (2010). Scare tactics to prevent you from exercising while sick. Triathlete Magazine Retrieved March 2010 from
http://www.active.com/triathlon/Articles/Scare_tactics_to_prevent_you_from_exercising_while_ill.htm.

(15) Mayo Clinic Staff. (n.d.). Symptoms: Myocarditis. MayoClinic.com. Retrieved March 2010 from
http://www.mayoclinic.com/health/myocarditis/DS00521/DSECTION=symptoms.

(16) Derby, S. (2009). Rough waters for triathletes after woman's drowning. CT The Cap Times. Retrieved June 2010 from
http://host.madison.com/ct/news/local/article_060d8b8c-41a6-5dd7-ad38-2453dcebc1ea.html.

(17) Choi, G., Kopplin, L. J., Tester, D. J., Will, M. L., Haglund, C. M. & Ackerman, M. J. (2004). Spectrum and frequency of cardiac channel defects in swimming-triggered arrhythmia syndromes. Circulation, 110(15), 2119-24.

(18) Zareba, W. & Cygankiewicz, I. (2008). Long QT syndrome and short QT syndrome. Progress in Cardiovascular Diseases, 51(3), 264-78.

Chapter 6: Breathe Easy
(1) Gerace, J. (Reviewer). (2009, June 9). Exercise-induced asthma. WebMD . Retrieved May 2010 from http://www.webmd.com/asthma/guide/exercise-induced-asthma.

(2) Miller, C., Calder-Becker, K. & Modave, F. (2010). Swimming-induced pulmonary edema in triathletes. American Journal of Emergency Medicine. Article in press.

Chapter 7: Don't Be Afraid of Sharks

(1) Anderson, C. (2005). Shark survivor: "I hit back". Shark Attack Survivors: News Archive. Shark Attack Surivors.com. Retrieved March 2010 from www.sharkattacksurvivors.com/shark_attack/viewtopic.php?f=7&t=291.

(2) Anonymous. (n.d.). Box Jellyfish. Amazing Australia.com.au. Retrieved April 2010 from http://www.amazingaustralia.com.au/animals/box_jellyfish_sea_wasp.htm.

(3) Woolgar, J., Cliff, G., Nair, R., Hafez, H. & Robbs, J. (2001). Shark attack: Review of 86 consecutive cases. The Journal of Trauma: Injury, Infection, and Critical Care, 50(5), 887-891.

(4) Selingo, J. (2002, June 13). How it works: When the shark doesn't bite. New York Times. Retrieved from nytimes.com.

(5) Friend, T. (n.d.). Back In The Water. ESPN. Retrieved February 2010 from http://sports.espn.go.com/espn/eticket/story?page=backinthewater.

(6) Ritter, E. (1998). Shark attacks - an ever intriguing puzzle. Shark Info. Retrieved February 2010 from http://www.sharkinfo.ch/SI2_98e/attacks1.html.

(7) Brenneka, A.l. (2005-2009). Sharkattackfile.com. (retrieved February 2010). Which article does this citation reference?

(8) Burgess, G. Menstruation. Florida Museum of Natural History, University of Florida. Retrieved February 2010 from http://www.flmnh.ufl.edu/fish/sharks/isaf/mens.htm.

(9) Ritter, E. (2005). Recommendations. Global Shark Attack File. Retrieved March 2010 from SharkAttackFile.net.

(10) Edmonds, M. (2008). 10 most dangerous places for shark attacks. HowStuffWorks.com. Retrieved March 2010 from www.animals.howstuffworks.com/fish/dangerous-place-shark-attack.htm.

(11) Lerman, I. (2002, June 2). New device aims to keep sharks away. The Daytona Beach News-Journal. Retrieved March 2010 from http://www.flmnh.ufl.edu/fish/sharks/innews/day092003.htm.

(12) Keet, A. Electrical shark repellant. Sharks.org. Retrieved February 2010 from http://www.Sharks.org.

Section 2:
Chapter 8: Love Your Wetsuit

(1) Lee, A. (2007). My wetsuit tried to kill me. Albert's tri life and times. Retrieved May 2010 from http://albertlee.wordpress.com/2007/05/23/my-wetsuit-tried-to-kill-me.

(2) Cordain, L. & Kopriva, R. (1991). Wetsuits, body density and swimming performance. British Journal of Sports Medicine, 25(1), 31-3.

(3) Tomikawa, M., Shimoyama, Y., & Nomura, T.J. (2008). Factors related to the advantageous effects of wearing a wetsuit during swimming at different submaximal velocity in triathletes . Journal of Science and Medicine in Sport, 11(4), 417-23.

(4) International Triathlon Union. (2008). ITU Competition rules. International Triathlon Union. Retrieved March 2010 from http://www.triathlon.org/docs/competition-rules-20080601-vf.pdf?ts=1268173069.

(5) USA Triathlon. (2010). USA Triathlon competitive rules. USA Triathlon. Retrieved March 2010 from http://assets.usoc.org/assets/documents/attached_file/filename/22589/usat_rules_03.01.10.pdf.

(6) Anonymous. (2010, April 13). Ironman announces U.S. rule amendments for 2011 season. Ironman.com. Retrieved July 2010 from
http://ironman.com/mediacenter/pressreleases/new-rules-to-take-effect-on-september-1-2010#axzz10fvlhgxb.
(7) USATriathlon.org. (2010, June 21). USA Triathlon adopts new wetsuit regulation. USA Triathlon.com. Retrieved July 2010 from
http://www.usatriathlon.org/new/2010/06/21/usa-triathlon-adopts-new-wetsuit-regulation/36693.

General Sources:
Peeling, P., Bishop, D., Landers, G. & Boone, T. (2005). Effect of swimming intensity on subsequent cycling and overall triathlon performance. British Journal of Sports Medicine, 39(12):960-4.
Jay, O., Christensen, J.P. & White, M.D. (2010). Human face-only immersion in cold water reduces maximal apnoeic times and stimulates ventilation. Experimental Physiology, 92(1), 197-206.
Mantoni, T., Belhage, B. & Pott, F.C. (2006). Survival in cold water. Physiological consequences of accidental immersion in cold water. Ugeskr Laeger, 168(38), 3203-5.
Tipton, M.J., Mekjavic, I.B. & Eglin, C.M. (2000). Permanence of the habituation of the initial responses to cold-water immersion in humans. European Journal of applied Physiology, 83(1), 17-21.
Peeling, P. & Landers, G. (2007). The effect of a one-piece competition speed suit on swimming performance and thermoregulation during a swim-cycle trial in triathletes. Journal of Science and Medicine in Sport, 10(5), 327-33.

Chapter 10: **Wild Water**
General Sources:
McDonald, A. (n.d.). To swim or not to swim: Swimming and water pollution. Powerbar.com. Retrieved June 2010 from http://www.powerbar.com/articles/58/to-swim-or-not-to-swim-swimming-and-water-pollution.aspx.
Negin, N. (2006, May). FAQs: Protecting the public from contaminated beachwater. Natural Resources Defense Council. Retrieved June 2010 from
http://72.32.110.154/media/pressreleases/060524a.asp.
Anonymous. (2010). Recreational water illness (RWI). Centers for Disease Control and Prevention. Retrieved June 2010 from
http://www.cdc.gov/healthywater/swimming/rwi.

Appendix C: **Summary of Triathlete deaths**
(1) Weinfuss, J.(2008). Tri-accidental tragedy Part III: Stories eerily similar. News Herald. Retrieved April 2010 from http://www.newsherald.com/sports/griffin-67429-barnett-first.html.
(2) The Associated Press. "Triathletes Body found in Lake Mercer" Retrieved from
http://www.nj.com/news/index.ssf/2008/07/triathletes_body_found_in_lake.htmt.(3) Van Derbeken, J. (2008). Swimmer, 63, dies during Alcatraz triathlon attempt. Retrieved March 2010 from http://articles.sfgate.com/2008-08-26/bay-area/17122396_1_triathlon-s-organizer-swimming-erin-williams.

(4) Anonymous. (2007, September 17). 55-year-old Madison man dies in triathlon at Devil's Lake. Channel3000.com. Retrieved May 2010 from http://www.channel3000.com/news/14135136/detail.html.

(5) Krishnan, S. (2008). Renton man dies during triathlon in Oregon. Seattle Times. Retrieved April 2010 from http://seattletimes.nwsource.com/html/localnews/2008025398_webtriathlete3om.html.

(6) Watte, K. (2008). Sadness over triathlete's death at Wickiup. KTXZ.com. Retrieved May 2010 from http://www.ktvz.com/Global/story.asp?s=8581852Shock.

(7) ESPN.com News Services. (2008). Haskins, Kemper earn U.S. berths after Iowa man dies in event. ESPN.com. Retrieved March 2010 from http://sports.espn.go.com/oly/news/story?id=3456299.

(8) Gross, C. (2008). Jim Goodman dies suddenly in triathlon. The Guillotine Forum: Talk Wrestling: College. Retrieved July 2010 from http://s7.zetaboards.com/The_Guillotine_Forum/topic/755967/1.

(9) Aschwanden, C. (2008, July 31). Deaths draw attention to triathlon swim. New York Times. Retrieved March 2010 from http://www.nytimes.com/2008/07/31/fashion/31fitness.html.

(10) Gregorian, C. B. (2009, June 4). Second anniversary of triathlete's death shines light on safety. Mynextrace.com. Retrieved April 2010 from http://www.mynextrace.com/index.php?name=News&file=article&sid=912 Triathlon.

(11) Jeff. (2007, August 9). Letter to the editor. Kevin M Hunt Foundation.org. Retrieved March 2010 from http://www.kevinmhuntfoundation.org/home/message-board/miscellaneous2/response-to-triathlon-death-of-kevin-hunt-at-innsbrook-on-06/23/07.

(12) Anonymous. (2008, May 10). Triathlon Death. News Channel 7. Retrieved May 2010 from http://www.wjhg.com/home/headlines/18835124.html.

(13) Daniel, M. (2007). Triathlete died of a heart attack. The Globe. Retrieved March 2010 from http://www.boston.com/news/local/massachusetts/articles/2007/07/10/triathlete_died_of_a_heart_attack.

(14) Anonymous. (2007, May 4). Chicago triathlete dies. Chicago Tribune. Retrieved April 2010 from http://featuresblogs.chicagotribune.com/features_julieshealthclub/2007/05/was_the_race_to.html.

(15) Times Wires. (2007, May 5).Triathlete died from drowning. St. Petersburg Times. Retrieved March 2010 from http://www.sptimes.com/2007/05/05/State/Dateline_Florida.shtml.

(16) Anonymous. (2008, July 28). Provo man dies while swimming in triathlon. Deseret News and Associated Press. Retrieved March 2010 from http://www.deseretnews.com/article/1,5143,700246513,00.html.

(17) Haggerty, R. & Held, T. (2009, July 13). Man who died in Pewaukee triathlon had lost 100 pounds in training. Journal Sentinel. Retrieved March 2010 from http://www.jsonline.com/news/waukesha/50617442.html.

(18) George, M. & Sorgi, J.(2009). Pewaukee triathlon drowning victim identified. Today's TMJ4 Milwaukee. Retrieved June 2010 from http://www.todaystmj4.com/news/local/50592947.html.

(19) Anonymous. (2009, July 12). Man drowns during Pewaukee Lake triathlon. Wisn.com. Retrieved from April 2010 from http://www.wisn.com/news/20033075/detail.html.

(20) ESPN. (2008). Coroner says NYC triathlete died of condition linked to high blood pressure. ESPN.com. Retrieved April 2010 from
http://sports.espn.go.com/oly/news/story?id=3669586.

(21) Glenn, M. (2008) Triathlete had years of experience in sport. Houston Chronicle. Retrieved May 2010 from
http://www.chron.com/disp/story.mpl/front/5753436.html.

(22) Anonymous. (2009, August 2). CEO of Deutsche Telekom Asia dies after swim leg at triathlon event. Red Sports. Retrieved March 2010 from
http://redsports.sg/2009/08/02/swimdeath-triathlon.

(23) Voon, T. (2009). CEO dies in triathlon. Straitstimes. Retrieved May 2010 from
http://www.straitstimes.com/Breaking%2BNews/Singapore/Story/STIStory_411710.html.

(24) Record Searchlight Staff. (2009, September 8). Alameda man dies in Mount Shasta triathlon. Redding.com. Retrieved May 2010 from
http://www.redding.com/news/2009/sep/08/alameda-man-dies-mount-shasta-triathlon.

(25) Record Searchlight Staff. (2009, September 26). Cause of death listed for triathlon swimmer. Redding.com: North state in brief. Retrieved May 2010 from
http://www.redding.com/news/2009/sep/26/north-state-in-brief-sept-26-2009/?partner=RSS.

(26) Daniel, M. (2007). Triathlete died of a heart attack. Boston Globe. Retrieved March 2010 from
http://www.boston.com/news/local/massachusetts/articles/2007/07/10/triathlete_died_of_a_heart_attack.

(27) Angier, D. (2009). Triathlete's family testifies in wrongful death case. Florida Freedom Newspapers. Retrieved May 2010 from
http://www.nwfdailynews.com/news/rice-18759-jurors-triathlon.html.

(28) Anonymous. (2009). Ironman not liable for death of amateur athlete federal jury finds. EverymanTri.com. Retrieved May 2010 from
http://www.everymantri.com/everyman_triathlon/2009/07/ironman-not-liable-for-death-of-amatuer-athlete-federal-jury-finds-.html.

(29) Hislop, K. (2009). Tragic death in Oshkosh Triathlon. NY Triathlon Examiner. Retrieved May 2010 from
http://www.examiner.com/x-16850-NY-Triathlon-Examiner~y2009m8d20-Tragic-death-in-Oshkosh-Triathlon-August-2009.

(30) Held, T. (2009). Memorializing a south shore triathlete. The Journal Sentinel. Retrieved May 2010 from http://www.jsonline.com/blogs/lifestyle/48153352.html.

(31) Justgiving.com. (2005). In Memory of Paul.
http://original.justgiving.com/pages/?pid=473768 London triathlon - In memory of Paul. (retrieved June 2010). Why is a personal page for donations being cited? It doesn't make sense and is not a source

(32) Voon, T. (2009). CEO dies during OSIM triathlon. The Straits Times. Retrieved May 2010 from
http://www.asiaone.com/News/the%2BStraits%2BTimes/Story/A1Story20090803-158636.html.

(33) Anonymous. (2009, August 28). Stroke caused Vazquez' death in Ironman triathlon. GMANewsTV.com. Retrieved June 2010 from
http://www.gmanews.tv/story/170960/stroke-caused-vazquez-death-in-ironman-triathlon.

(34) Perry, N. (2003). Hydrogen-power innovator dies in triathlon. The Seattle Times. Retrieved July 2010 from
http://community.seattletimes.nwsource.com/archive/?date=20030809&slug=obitveith09e.

(35) Anonymous. (2008, May 1). Veith v. Xterra Wetsuits LLC. Court of Appeals of Washington, Division 3. Retrieved July 2010 from
http://caselaw.findlaw.com/wa-court-of-appeals/1404393.html.

(36) Anonymous. (2009, September 1). Swimmer's death forces Ironman into review. Kelowna Daily Courier. Retrieved July 2010 from
http://www.kelownadailycourier.ca/includes/datafiles/print.php?id=208555&title=Swimmer%92s%20ddeat%20forces%20Ironman%20into%20review.

(37) Hospedales, R. (2010) Death at Ironman Canada Ruled Accidental. Retrieved October 2010 from http://triathlonmagazine.ca/2010/02/sections/news/accidental-death-at-ironman-canada.

(38) Kinkade, S. (2009, September 9). Competitor dies during Tinman Triathlon swim. Mt. Shasta News. Retrieved April 2010 from
http://www.mtshastanews.com/news/x837457625/Competitor-dies-during-Tinman-Triathlon-swim.

(39) Weinfuss, J. (2008). Tri-accidental tragedy Part I: Triple tragedy. News Herald. Retrieved March 2010 from
http://www.newsherald.com/sports/water-67303-swim-gulf.html.

PHOTO CREDITS

Cover photo: dpa – Picture Alliance
Photos: see individual photos
Cover design: Sabine Groten

INDEX

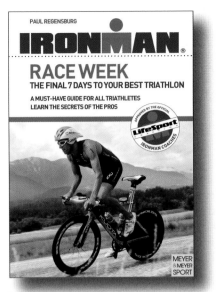

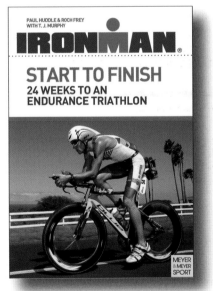